Creating Cool Web Pages with HTML

by Dave Taylor

Creating Cool Web Pages with HTML

by Dave Taylor

IDG Books Worldwide, Inc.
An International Data Group Company

Foster City, CA ◆ Chicago, IL ◆ Indianapolis, IN ◆ Braintree, MA ◆ Dallas, TX

Creating Cool Web Pages with HTML

Published by
IDG Books Worldwide, Inc.
An International Data Group Company
919 E. Hillsdale Blvd.
Suite 400
Foster City, CA 94404

Library of Congress Catalog Card No.: 95-76828

ISBN: 1-56884-454-9

Printed in the United States of America

10 9 8 7 6 5 4 3 2 1

1B/QW/QW/ZV

Distributed in the United States by IDG Books Worldwide, Inc.

Distributed by Macmillan Canada for Canada; by Computer and Technical Books for the Caribbean Basin; by Contemporanea de Ediciones for Venezuela; by Distribuidora Cuspide for Argentina; by CITEC for Brazil; by Ediciones ZETA S.C.R. Ltda. for Peru; by Editorial Limusa SA for Mexico; by Transworld Publishers Limited in the United Kingdom and Europe; by Al-Maiman Publishers & Distributors for Saudi Arabia; by Simron Pty. Ltd. for South Africa; by IDG Communications (HK) Ltd. for Hong Kong; by Toppan Company Ltd. for Japan; by Addison Wesley Publishing Company for Korea; by Longman Singapore Publishers Ltd. for Singapore, Malaysia, Thailand, and Indonesia; by Unalis Corporation for Taiwan; by WS Computer Publishing Company, Inc. for the Philippines; by WoodsLane Pty. Ltd. for Australia; by WoodsLane Enterprises Ltd. for New Zealand.

For general information on IDG Books Worldwide's books in the U.S., including information on discounts and premiums, contact IDG Books Worldwide at 800-434-3422 or 415-655-3000.

For information on where to purchase IDG Books Worldwide's books outside the U.S., contact IDG Books Worldwide at 415-655-3021 or fax 415-655-3295.

For information on translations, contact Marc Jeffrey Mikulich, Director, Foreign & Subsidiary Rights, at IDG Books Worldwide, 415-655-3018 or fax 415-655-3295.

For sales inquiries and special prices for bulk quantities, write to the address above or call IDG Books Worldwide at 415-655-3200.

For information on using IDG Books Worldwide's books in the classroom, or ordering examination copies, contact Jim Kelly at 800-434-2086.

For authorization to photocopy items for corporate, personal, or educational use, please contact Copyright Clearance Center, 222 Rosewood Drive, Danvers, MA 01923, or fax 508-750-4470.

Some of the screen shots in this book are based on Microsoft® Windows® 95 made public by Microsoft Corporation as of March 1995. Because this information was made public before the final release of Windows 95, the final interface may be different than illustrated herein. We encourage you to visit your local bookstore after Windows 95 is released for updated books on Windows 95.

 is a registered trademark under exclusive license to IDG Books Worldwide, Inc., from International Data Group, Inc.

About the Author

Dave Taylor

Dave Taylor has been involved with the Internet since 1980, when he first logged in as an undergraduate student at the University of California, San Diego. Since then he's been a research scientist at Hewlett-Packard Laboratories in Palo Alto, California, a software and hardware reviews editor for *SunWorld* magazine, and an interface design consultant for XALT Software. He is president of Intuitive Systems in Palo Alto.

So far, Dave has designed more than 500 Web pages. He has published more than 750 articles on Internet, UNIX, Macintosh, and other computing topics. His books include *Global Software* and *Teach Yourself Unix in a Week*. He coauthored *The Internet Business Guide*. He is well known as the author of the Elm Mail System and, more recently, the Embot mail autoresponder program.

He holds a Masters degree in Educational Computing from Purdue University and an undergraduate degree in Computer Science at the University of California, San Diego.

On the Web, Dave has created The Internet Mall™ and the Purdue University Online Writing Laboratory and is busy developing a Tintin Web information space and too many other projects to list!

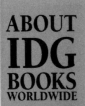

Welcome to the world of IDG Books Worldwide.

IDG Books Worldwide, Inc., is a subsidiary of International Data Group, the world's largest publisher of computer-related information and the leading global provider of information services on information technology. IDG was founded more than 25 years ago and now employs more than 7,500 people worldwide. IDG publishes more than 235 computer publications in 67 countries (see listing below). More than 60 million people read one or more IDG publications each month.

Launched in 1990, IDG Books Worldwide is today the #1 publisher of best-selling computer books in the United States. We are proud to have received 8 awards from the Computer Press Association in recognition of editorial excellence, and our best-selling ...*For Dummies*™ series has more than 17 million copies in print with translations in 25 languages. IDG Books Worldwide, through a recent joint venture with IDG's Hi-Tech Beijing, became the first U.S. publisher to publish a computer book in the People's Republic of China. In record time, IDG Books Worldwide has become the first choice for millions of readers around the world who want to learn how to better manage their businesses.

Our mission is simple: Every one of our books is designed to bring extra value and skill-building instructions to the reader. Our books are written by experts who understand and care about our readers. The knowledge base of our editorial staff comes from years of experience in publishing, education, and journalism — experience which we use to produce books for the '90s. In short, we care about books, so we attract the best people. We devote special attention to details such as audience, interior design, use of icons, and illustrations. And because we use an efficient process of authoring, editing, and desktop publishing our books electronically, we can spend more time ensuring superior content and spend less time on the technicalities of making books.

You can count on our commitment to deliver high-quality books at competitive prices on topics consumers want to read about. At IDG Books Worldwide, we value quality, and we have been delivering quality for more than 25 years. You'll find no better book on a subject than an IDG book.

John J. Kilcullen

John Kilcullen
President and CEO
IDG Books Worldwide, Inc.

IDG Books Worldwide, Inc., is a subsidiary of International Data Group, the world's largest publisher of computer-related information and the leading global provider of information services on information technology. International Data Group publishes over 235 computer publications in 67 countries. More than sixty million people read one or more International Data Group publications each month. The officers are Patrick J. McGovern, Founder and Board Chairman; Kelly Conlin, President; Jim Casella, Chief Operating Officer. International Data Group's publications include: **ARGENTINA'S** Computerworld Argentina, Infoworld Argentina; **AUSTRALIA'S** Computerworld Australia, Computer Living, Australian PC World, Australian Macworld, Network World, Mobile Business Australia, Publish!, Reseller, IDG Sources; **AUSTRIA'S** Computerwelt Oesterreich, PC Test; **BELGIUM'S** Data News (CW); **BOLIVIA'S** Computerworld; **BRAZIL'S** Computerworld, Connections, Game Power, Mundo Unix, PC World, Publish, Super Game; **BULGARIA'S** Computerworld Bulgaria, PC & Mac World Bulgaria, Network World Bulgaria; **CANADA'S** CIO Canada, Computerworld Canada, InfoCanada, Network World Canada, Reseller; **CHILE'S** Computerworld Chile, Informatica; **COLOMBIA'S** Computerworld Colombia, PC World; **COSTA RICA'S** PC World; **CZECH REPUBLIC'S** Computerworld, Elektronika, PC World; **DENMARK'S** Communications World, Computerworld Danmark, Computerworld Focus, Macintosh Produktkatalog, Macworld Danmark, PC World Danmark, PC Produktguide, Tech World, Windows World; **ECUADOR'S** PC World Ecuador; **EGYPT'S** Computerworld (CW) Middle East, PC World Middle East; **FINLAND'S** MikroPC, Tietoviikko, Tietoverkko; **FRANCE'S** Distributique, GOLDEN MAC, InfoPC, Le Guide du Monde Informatique, Le Monde Informatique, Telecoms & Reseaux; **GERMANY'S** Computerwoche, Computerwoche Focus, Computerwoche Extra, Electronic Entertainment, Gamepro, Information Management, Macwelt, Netzwelt, PC Welt, Publish, Publish; **GREECE'S** Publish & Macworld; **HONG KONG'S** Computerworld Hong Kong, PC World Hong Kong; **HUNGARY'S** Computerworld SZT, PC World; **INDIA'S** Computers & Communications; **INDONESIA'S** Info Komputer; **IRELAND'S** ComputerScope; **ISRAEL'S** Beyond Windows, Computerworld Israel, Multimedia, PC World Israel; **ITALY'S** Computerworld Italia, Lotus Magazine, Macworld Italia, Networking Italia, PC Shopping Italy, PC World Italia; **JAPAN'S** Computerworld Today, Information Systems World, Macworld Japan, Nikkei Personal Computing, SunWorld Japan, Windows World; **KENYA'S** East African Computer News; **KOREA'S** Computerworld Korea, Macworld Korea, PC World Korea; **LATIN AMERICA'S** GamePro; **MALAYSIA'S** Computerworld Malaysia, PC World Malaysia; **MEXICO'S** Compu Edicion, Compu Manufactura, Computacion/Punto de Venta, Computerworld Mexico, MacWorld, Mundo Unix, PC World, Windows; **THE NETHERLANDS'** Computer! Totaal, Computable (CW), LAN Magazine, Lotus Magazine, MacWorld; **NEW ZEALAND'S** Computer Buyer, Computerworld New Zealand, Network World, New Zealand PC World; **NIGERIA'S** PC World Africa; **NORWAY'S** Computerworld Norge, Lotusworld Norge, Macworld Norge, Maxi Data, Networld, PC World Ekspress, PC World Nettverk, PC World Norge, PC World's Produktguide, Publish& Multimedia World, Student Data, Unix World, Windowsworld; **PAKISTAN'S** PC World Pakistan; **PANAMA'S** PC World Panama; **PERU'S** Computerworld Peru, PC World; **PEOPLE'S REPUBLIC OF CHINA'S** China Computerworld, China Infoworld, China PC Info Magazine, Computer Fan, PC World China, Electronics International, Electronics Today/Multimedia World, Electronic Product World, China Network World, Software World Magazine, Telecom Product World; **PHILIPPINES'** Computerworld Philippines, PC Digest (PCW); **POLAND'S** Computerworld Poland, Computerworld Special Report, Networld, PC World/Komputer, Sunworld; **PORTUGAL'S** Cerebro/PC World, Correio Informatico/Computerworld, MacIn; **ROMANIA'S** Computerworld, PC World, Telecom Romania; **RUSSIA'S** Computerworld-Moscow, Mir – PK (PCW), Sety (Networks); **SINGAPORE'S** Computerworld Southeast Asia, PC World Singapore; **SLOVENIA'S** Monitor Magazine; **SOUTH AFRICA'S** Computer Mail (CIO),Computing S.A.,Network World S.A., Software World; **SPAIN'S** Advanced Systems, Amiga World, Computerworld Espana, Communicaciones World, Macworld Espana, NeXTWORLD, Super Juegos Magazine (GamePro), PC World Espana, Publish; **SWEDEN'S** Attack, ComputerSweden, Corporate Computing, Macworld, Mikrodatorn, Natverk & Kommunikation, PC World, CAP & Design, Datalngenjoren, Maxi Data,Windows World; **SWITZERLAND'S** Computerworld Schweiz, Macworld Schweiz, PC Tip; **TAIWAN'S** Computerworld Taiwan, PC World Taiwan; **THAILAND'S** Thai Computerworld; **TURKEY'S** Computerworld Monitor, Macworld Turkiye, PC World Turkiye; **UKRAINE'S** Computerworld, Computers+Software Magazine; **UNITED KINGDOM'S** Computing /Computerworld, Connexion/Network World, Lotus Magazine, Macworld, Open Computing/Sunworld; **UNITED STATES'** Advanced Systems, AmigaWorld, Cable in the Classroom, CD Review, CIO, Computerworld, Computerworld Client/Server Journal, Digital Video, DOS World, Electronic Entertainment Magazine (E2), Federal Computer Week, Game Hits, GamePro, IDG Books Worldwide, Infoworld, Laser Event, Macworld, Maximize, Multimedia World, Network World, PC Letter, PC World, Publish, SWATPro, Video Event; **URUGUAY'S** PC World Uruguay; **VENEZUELA'S** Computerworld Venezuela, PC World; **VIETNAM'S** PC World Vietnam.
05/17/95

Dedication

To the ever-cool Judi.

Credits

Publisher
Karen A. Bluestein

Acquisitions Manager
Gregory Croy

Acquisitions Editor
Ellen L. Camm

Brand Manager
Melisa M. Duffy

Editorial Director
Mary Bednarek

Editorial Managers
Mary C. Corder
Andy Cummings

Editorial Executive Assistant
Jodi Lynn Semling

Editorial Assistant
Nate Holdread

Production Director
Beth Jenkins

Supervisor of Project Coordination
Cindy L. Phipps

Pre-Press Coordinator
Steve Peake

Associate Pre-Press Coordinator
Tony Augsburger

Media/Archive Coordinator
Paul Belcastro

Project Editor
Corbin Collins

Editor
Kathy Simpson

Technical Reviewer
David Elderbrock

Project Coordinator
Valery Bourke

Production Staff
Gina Scott
Carla C. Radzikinas
Patricia R. Reynolds
Dwight Ramsey
Theresa Sánchez-Baker
Robert Springer
Cameron Booker
Maridee Ennis

Proofreader
Jennifer Kaufeld

Indexer
Sharon Hilgenberg

Book Design
Jo Payton

Cover Design
Three 8 Creative Group

Acknowledgments

No writing project can be done while the author is locked in a room, though if the room had a good Net connection, we might be able to negotiate something! Seriously, a number of Internet folk have proven invaluable as I've written this book, some for their direct help, and others for simply having produced some wickedly cool Web pages that helped inspire me when things were moving a bit slowly. Chief among those is the almost omniscient **James Armstrong** who helped me verify the internal details of the more obscure HTML tags, and technical editor **David Elderbrock** who not only helped out with some puzzling Web forms but also helped keep me honest throughout. My editor **Corbin Collins** at IDG Books continually offered valuable suggestions that helped me fine tune the prose herein. And the gangsta' trio of **Kevin Savetz, David Geller,** and **Tai Jin** also helped with their insight on page design and Web graphics layout, as well as suggestions for cool Web sites not to miss. Thanks to **Tim Stanley** for preparing the disk in the back of the book and to **Maridee Ennis** and **Cameron Booker** for making the book look so nice.

Adobe Systems, Macromedia, Pixar, and **Broderbund** were most generous with their assistance; many of the graphics presented in this book were created by **Photoshop, Illustrator, Freehand, Typestyler, Typestry** and other top-notch commercial applications on the Macintosh. Screenshots were done with **Capture** and the book was written mostly on an **Apple PowerBook Duo 210**, with everything verified with the **Centris 650** on my desk. Shareware gets a nod too: **Graphic Converter** and **GIFconverter** both proved helpful for ensuring that the images were in the correct form, and **Transparency** made 'em transparent. **MacWeb, Mosaic,** and **Netscape** were all quite capable Web browsers, although I prefer MacWeb simply because it's the smallest of the bunch.

A special thanks also goes to the fledgling **Metropolitan Data Networks** in Lafayette, Indiana, for its assistance and reliable PPP connectivity to the rest of the Net from my home at Purdue University, and to **Pete and the gang at Java Roaster** for a pleasant working environment and a great cup of latté too. Thanks to **IndyNet** in Indianapolis for making sure my files and e-mail messages actually got to my editor. The entire contents of this book were sent to my editor via the **Internet**.

Finally, warm hugs to **Linda, Jasmine,** and **Karma** for ensuring that I took sufficient breaks to avoid carpal tunnel syndrome or any of the other hazards of overly intense typing. The time off-line would be a lot less fun without ya!

(The Publisher would like to give special thanks to **Patrick J. McGovern**, without whom this book would not have been possible.)

Web Pages Used in This Book

You'll find the cool Web pages featured on our cover at the following URLs:

HotWired
http://www.hotwired.com/Login/index.html

Greenpeace® International
http://www.greenpeace.org/

The WeLL
http://www.well.com/

The White House
http://www.whitehouse.gov/

The image of the HotWired home page is used by permission of HotWired Ventures LLC. Greenpeace is a registered trademark of Greenpeace, Incorporated. The WeLL is a registered service mark of Whole Earth Lectronic Link, Incorporated. WeLL image © by WinslowCo Well.

The author and the publisher would like to acknowledge the following Internet Web sites for the use of their Web pages in screen shot images in this book.

NCSA What's New Page
http://www.ncsa.uiuc.edu/SDG/Software/Mosaic/Docs/whats-new.html

James C. Armstrong
ftp://ftp.netcom.com/pub/jc/jca/homepage.html

Computer Literacy Bookshops of California
http://www.clbooks.com/

PC Week Online
http://www.ziff.com/~pcweek
PC Week® Ziff-Davis Publishing Co.

Wentworth Gallery
http://wentworth-art.com
Illustrations by George Courage and Tony Valletti

Traveling Software
http://www.halcyon.com/travsoft/

Chris's World
http://128.172.69.103/bullet.html

W3C
http://www.w3.org
W3C and the W3C logo are trademarks of MIT.

Yahoo
http://yahoo.com

Lycos
http://lycos.cs.cmu.edu/
Lycos © Carnegie Mellon University

Island Puzzler Bookstore
http://adware.com/adware/puzzler/bookstore.html

WebCrawler
http://webcrawler.cs.washington.edu/WebCrawler/WebQuery.html

ElNet Galaxy
http://www.einet.net/

GNN Home Page
http://gnn.com/gnn/GNNhome.html

Yanoff's Internet Services page
http://www.uwm.edu/Mirror/inet.services.html

Netscape What's New Page
http://home.mcom.com/home/whats-new.html
Netscape and Netscape Navigator are trademarks of Netscape Communications
Corporation

Tarot Information
http://cad.ucla.edu/repository/useful/tarot.html

The Living City
http://www.cadvision.com/top.html
The Living City and Global Petroleum Center are trademarks

Global On-Line Directory
http://www.cityscape.co.uk/gold/indexdir.html

City.Net
http://www.city.net/

Inter-Links Internet Access
http://alpha.acast.nova.edu/start.html
Inter-Links™ © 1994 by Robert Kabakoff and Nova Southeastern University

Web of Wonder
http://www.digimark.net/wow

The InterNIC Directory of Directories
http://ds.internic.net/ds/dsdirofdirs.html

The Internet Mall™
http://www.mecklerweb.com/imall/

Open Market's Commercial Site Index
http://www.directory.net/
Open Market is a trademark of Open Market, Incorporated

Apollo Advertising
http://apollo.co.uk/

BizWeb
http://www.bizweb.com/

Product.Com
http://www.product.com/

MecklerWeb
http://www.mecklerweb.com/
© 1995 Meckler Media Corporation, 20 Ketchum Street, Westport, CT 06880;
info@mecklermedia.com

Contents at a Glance

Table of Contents

Foreword

Just the other day, I was roaming through the halls of the Louvre, looking at great works of art such as the *Mona Lisa*. An hour before, I had toured the exhibits of the University of California at Berkeley's Museum of Paleontology and learned about Dilophosaurs from a well-versed professor. And just a short while before that, I previewed Disney's upcoming summer flicks before actual movie audiences would. The remarkable thing about all these feats was that I accomplished them without ever leaving my home (or workstation, for that matter). The killer application of the network-of-networks is the World Wide Web, and you're nobody unless you have a cool home page on the Web.

Sporting the first truly user-friendly multimedia features for the Internet, the WWW represented about 1 percent of all Internet traffic in 1993. In 1994, it grew to 12 percent of all traffic and is now at a sky-rocketing 20 percent. A year ago there were 1,265 estimated Web Sites; today there are nearly 20,000!

As further evidence of rapid growth, most of the commercial online services opened their doors to the Web, with Prodigy leading the pack in mid-January 1995. Since then, nearly half a million Prodigy users have grabbed the Web browser software needed to enjoy this graphically intense corner of the Internet. When Microsoft ships Windows 95, another 20 to 30 million users could be just a click away from becoming Web surfers.

A year ago I had but a few Web sites in my Internet Services List and had barely trod into the realm myself. Today, my list is growing almost exclusively as Web sites. As a further testimonial, I am now employed as a Web Developer for SpectraCom, Incorporated in Milwaukee.

The future has arrived, and Dave Taylor has created a book to help newbie Web developers (such as myself!) design cool web pages in what once was a desert but is now an oasis of information and enjoyment. Dave is well known for providing the Internet with valuable information sources and tools, such as the Elm Mail System and the Internet Mall, and his trustworthy experience will once again be valuable in aiding university eggheads, corporate suits, and home-grown fanatics to exploit the capabilities of the Web and HTML.

— Scott Yanoff

Scott Yanoff is famous on the Net for creating and maintaining the valuable Internet Services List, a.k.a. Yanoff's List (which you can visit at `http://www.uwm.edu/Mirror/inet.services.html`*)*

Introduction

This is the Introduction. It answers questions like: Who should buy this book? What's covered? What's not? How do I read this book? Why should I read this book?

Lots of cool stuff is covered in *Creating Cool Web Pages with HTML*, starting with an introduction to the World Wide Web and its documents and ending with image maps, forms, and other sophsticated uses of HTML.

Welcome!

"Wow! Another Internet book. What makes this one different?"

That's a fair question. I designed this Introduction to answer that question. I want you to be confident that *Creating Cool Web Pages with HTML* will meet your needs as well as provide fun and interesting reading.

What This Book Is About

In a nutshell, *Creating Cool Web Pages with HTML* is an introduction to HTML. HTML stands for *HyperText Markup Language*, and it is the markup language that enables you to create and publish your own multimedia documents on the World Wide Web. Millions of users on the Internet and online services such as America Online, CompuServe, and Prodigy are learning how to use the visually exciting World Wide Web from within Mosaic, Netscape, Cello, winWeb, MacWeb, and a growing list of other programs.

You can create attractive documents that are right on the cutting edge of interactive publishing. That's why I went through the pain of learning HTML. For me, learning was hit or miss, because the only references I could find were confusing online documents written by programmers and computer types. For you, it will be easier. By reading this book and experimenting with the winWeb software and samples included on the floppy disk, you can learn not only the nuts and bolts of HTML but also how to design and create useful, attractive Web documents and spread the word about them on the Net.

To make things even more fun in this book, I pop into various cool and interesting Web sites and show you the HTML code used to create those pages. In the end, cool Web documents aren't necessarily those that have extensive or pretty graphics. With a little verve and some witty prose, you'll see how you can present purely textual information via the Web in a way that's interesting, visually engaging, helpful, and fun — in other words, *cool*.

Those things are what this book is all about.

What This Book Isn't About

This book doesn't introduce you to or tell you how you can get on the Internet. (It does, however, include a brief and painless introduction to the World Wide Web.) If you seek detailed information about the Net or want to find out how to "get on" it, you can find many interesting and useful books from IDG Books and elsewhere on those topics. And because of space restraints, this book *introduces* some very advanced HTML topics — such as how to create forms or build HTML pages on-the-fly — but doesn't explore them in depth.

Instead, *Creating Cool Web Pages with HTML* is a fun introduction to the art and science of creating interesting Web documents that you'll be proud of and that other users will want to visit and explore.

How This Book Is Organized

Chapter 1: "What Is a Web Page?" covers the basics of markup languages, sketches out how the Web works, and discusses the different types of information found in documents on the Net.

Chapter 2: "URLs: What They Are and How to Use Them" defines Uniform Resource Locators and explains how to make them for your own use. The chapter also includes brief discussions of FTP, Gopher, and e-mail as they relate to URL construction.

Chapter 3: "Basic HTML" discusses the basics of creating HTML documents, including head and body information, meaningful page titles, paragraph and section-head marks, horizontal rules, and other layout elements.

Chapter 4: "Text Styles" explains how to add boldface, italics, and other types of emphasis to HTML text.

Chapter 5: "Lists and Special Characters" discusses various types of lists for Web documents, including numbered lists, bullet lists, and definition lists. The chapter also explains how to add comments to your Web documents that other users cannot see with their viewers.

Chapter 6: "Adding Pointers and Hot Links" explains how to insert HTML pointers to other Web or Internet resources into your Web pages and explains how to include pointers to graphics and illustrations. The chapter builds on the earlier URL explanation provided in Chapter 2.

Chapter 7: "Internal Document References" explains how to add a table of contents to a large Web document and how to use that table as hot links which enable people to jump to specific spots in the same Web document.

Chapter 8: "Jazzing Up Web Pages" shows how to enhance Web pages with multimedia. It explains how to create and edit graphical images, audio, and even video clips. This is the only chapter that contains platform-specific info: graphical editors and GIF translators for Mac, PC/Windows, and UNIX systems.

Chapter 9: "The Netscape HTML Extensions" explores the many cool additions to HTML that are supported in the Netscape Navigator Web browser. This chapter also shows how to design Web pages that are not only cool and slick when viewed within Netscape but are also still visually interesting and attractive when seen within Web browsers, such as winWeb, which don't support the additional capabilities.

Chapter 10: "Searching, Finding, and Being Found" explains how Web search engines work and how to design your material so that it will be useful when indexed by Web-Crawler, Lycos, Yahoo, and the many other search applications available on the Web. The chapter also shows you how to have your new Web site included in these indexes.

Chapter 11: "Announcing Your Site" addresses avenues for announcing and promoting your new site on the Net and for generating visitors.

Chapter 12: "Where to Next?" provides an introduction to graphical maps (called ISMAPs in HTML), forms and database queries, a list of items that will change when HTML 2 is released, and so on. The chapter also includes URL pointers to online documents that define the latest specifications and applications.

Appendix A: "Glossary" defines most Web-related terms used in this book.

Appendix B: "HTML Quick Reference" provides a nice summary in one place of all the HTML tags and options explained throughout the book.

Text Conventions Used in This Book

Stuff you type appears in bold, like this: **something you actually type.**

Filenames, names of machines on the Net, and directories appear in a special typeface, like the following one, which lets visitors sign a White House guest book:

```
http://www.whitehouse.gov/White_House/html/Guest_Book.html
```

HTML-formatted text appears in the same special typeface, like this:

```
<HTML>
<TITLE>How to Write Cool Web Pages</TITLE>
<IMG SRC="intro.gif" ALT="How To Write Cool Web Pages">
```

I use three icons in this book:

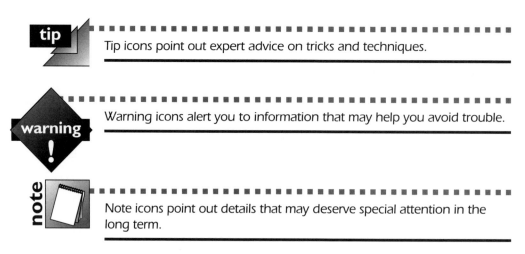

tip Tip icons point out expert advice on tricks and techniques.

warning ! Warning icons alert you to information that may help you avoid trouble.

note Note icons point out details that may deserve special attention in the long term.

Whom This Book Is For

Even if you don't have a connection to the Internet, you can use this book and software to learn HTML and the techniques of creating cool Web pages. All you need are a simple text editor, such as Notepad, which comes with Windows, and winWeb, the fine freeware browser from EINet that is conveniently packaged on the disk in the back of the book. Or you can use any of several other Web browsers available from the Net, such as NCSA Mosaic or Netscape.

If you're already online and have a Web browser hooked up, you can easily explore local files (files on your computer) and then log on to explore the many fascinating examples of Web-page design on the Internet itself.

A Sneak Peek at Some Actual HTML

Are you curious about what this HTML stuff looks like? The following figure shows what a portion of the outline for this book might look like as a simple HTML document, as seen in Netscape.

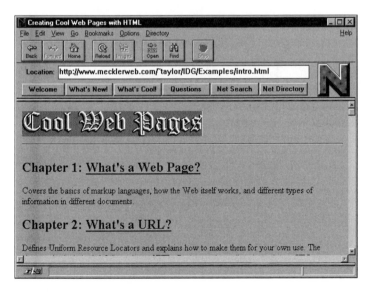

Figure 0-1: A Web page viewed in Netscape.

The following is the raw HTML document that lurks behind Figure 0-1:

```
<HTML>
<HEAD>
<TITLE>Creating Cool Web Pages with HTML</TITLE>
</HEAD><BODY>
<IMG SRC="intro.gif" ALT="Creating Cool Web Pages with HTML">
<HR>
<H2>Chapter 1: <A HREF="chap1.html">What's a Web Page?</A></H2>
Covers the basics of markup languages, how the Web itself works, and
different types of information in different documents.
<H2>Chapter 2: <A HREF="chap2.html">What's a URL?</A></H2>
Defines Uniform Resource Locators and explains how to make them for
your own use. The chapter also includes brief discussions of FTP, Gopher,
and e-mail as they relate to URL construction.
<H2>Chapter 3: <A HREF="chap3.html">Basic Web Markup:
HTML</A></H2>
Discusses the basics of creating an HTML document, including head and
body information, meaningful page titles, paragraph and section-head
marks, horizontal rules, and other layout information.
<P>
<I>And much, much more!</I>
</BODY>
</HTML>
</HTML>
```

By the time you're halfway through this book, you'll be able to whip up the kind of material in Figure 0-1 yourself, guaranteed. And by the time you *finish* this book, you'll know other ways to organize information to make creating Web versions of print material easy. You'll also learn why the particular HTML layout seen in Figure 0-1 isn't necessarily the best way to present information in a hyperlinked environment such as the Web.

Want to contact the author? Send e-mail to taylor@netcom.com or visit my home page on the Web at http://www.mecklerweb.com/~taylor.

The home page for this book is http://www.mecklerweb.com/~taylor/IDG/coolweb.html

If you're ready, let's go!

What Is a
Web Page?

This chapter covers the basics of the Web, shows
how information pointers help organize information, and
illustrates how Web browsers can simplify FTP, Gopher, and
other Internet services.

In this chapter

- ❑ Linear media
- ❑ Hypermedia
- ❑ Cool spots on the Web
- ❑ Non-HTML information on the Web

It's important for you to have a basic understanding of what a "web"
of information is all about right off the bat. Before we look at the basics
of creating cool Web pages, therefore, let's take a close look at what
the Web is, how it works, and what HTML itself is all about. I promise
to be brief!

What Is the Web Anyway?

To understand the World Wide Web, it's a good idea to first consider how information is organized in print media. Print media, I think, is a fair model for the Web and how it's all organized, though others may feel that adventure games, movies, TV, or other information publishing media are better suited for comparison to the Web.

Linear media

Think about the physical and organizational characteristics of this book for a second. What characteristics are most notable? The book has discrete units of information: pages. The pages are conceptually organized into chapters. The chapters are bound together to comprise the book itself. In some sense, what you have in your hands is a collection of pages organized in a format conducive to your reading them from first page to last. However, there's no reason why you can't riffle through the pages and create your own strategy for navigating this information.

Are you still with me? I call the book example *linear information organization*. Like movies, most books are organized with the expectation that you'll start at the beginning and end at the end.

Hypermedia

Imagine that instead of physically turning the page, you can simply touch a spot at the bottom of each page — a forward arrow — to flip to the next page. Touching a different spot — a back arrow — moves you to the preceding page. Further, imagine that when you look at the table of contents, you can touch the description of a chapter to immediately flip directly to the page where the chapter begins*. Touch a third spot — a small picture of a dictionary — and move to another book entirely.

Such a model is called *hypermedia* or *hypertext*, terms coined by mid-20th century computer visionaries, most notably Ted Nelson in his book *Computer Lib*. Some things become apparent in this more dynamic approach to organization. One immediate benefit is that the topical index suddenly becomes *really* helpful; by being able to touch an item of interest, whether explanatory narrative or descriptive reference material, you can use the same book as a reference work in addition to the linearly organized tutorial that it's intended to offer. It's like the best of two worlds — the linear flow of an audio or video tape, and the instant access of a music CD.

* This is how many people would like to read books, right?

Another benefit of hypertext involves footnotes. Consider the footnote a few paragraphs back. Footnote text doesn't have to clutter up the bottom of the page; with hypertext, you merely touch the asterisk or footnote number in the text, and a tiny page pops up to display the footnote.

One more idea: you can touch an illustration to zoom into a larger version of that illustration or maybe even convert the illustration to an animated sequence.

What makes the Web really fun and interesting is the fact that the pages of information you connect to can reside on a variety of systems throughout the world. The pages themselves can be quite complex (and, ideally, cool and attractive) documents. Imagine: instead of writing "You can see the White House Web page to learn more," leaving everyone stranded and unsure of how to proceed, Web documents enable direct *links,* so readers can click on the highlighted words in the sentence and immediately zoom to the White House.

Cool spots on the Web

Figure 1-1 shows a typical text-only Web document that you'll explore later in the book. Notice particularly the underlined words, each of which actually is a link to another Web document elsewhere in the Internet.

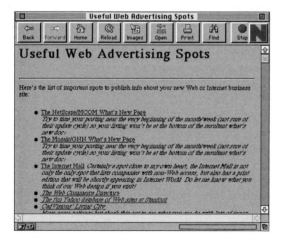

Figure 1-1: Some interesting spots to visit on the Internet.

If you're on the Internet, and you click on the phrase <u>The Mosaic/GNN What's New Page</u>, you travel (electronically) to the National Center for Supercomputing Applications (NCSA) at the University of Illinois in Urbana-Champaign, as shown in Figure 1-2.

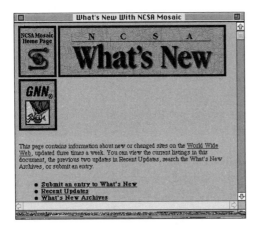

Figure 1-2: The NCSA What's New page.

What do I mean by *click on*? I'm sure you already know: Clicking is "touching" a spot on the screen; place the mouse pointer over a word or picture and then press the mouse button. Clicking works whether you're running on a Macintosh, a Windows machine, or a UNIX workstation running X Windows.

What makes all this so compelling for me (and for millions of other users) is the fact that there aren't thousands or tens of thousands of Web documents, there are *millions of them* — so many, in fact, that no one has ever visited all of them. So many documents are available that finding information is perhaps the single greatest challenge on the Internet. (Whew — I almost wrote *on the information highway*. I'll try to avoid that cliché, even though the metaphor actually can be helpful in considering traffic patterns, connection speeds, and various other arcana.)

Non-HTML Web Information

Although it's certainly true that much of the information on the World Wide Web consists of rich multimedia documents written in HTML specifically for the enjoyment of Web readers, the majority of documents actually come from other types of information-publishing services on the Internet. These documents are presented in the most attractive formats possible within the Web browsers themselves.

FTP

The simplest of the different information services on the Internet is FTP (File Transfer Protocol). FTP has been around for a long time, long before the Web was envisioned. Traditionally, working with FTP is a pain, and the interface has always been only a tiny step away from programming the computer directly. For example, from a UNIX host, you would have to type the following sequence of steps to connect to the Digital Equipment Corporation FTP archive called `gatekeeper.dec.com` (user input is in boldface):

```
% ftp gatekeeper.dec.com
Connected to gatekeeper.dec.com.
220 gatekeeper.dec.com FTP server (Version 5.97 Fri May 6 14:44:16 PDT
1994) ready.
Name (gatekeeper.dec.com:taylor): anonymous
331 Guest login ok, send ident as password.
Password:taylor@netcom.com
230 Guest login ok, access restrictions apply.
ftp> dir hypertext
200 PORT command successful.
150 Opening ASCII mode data connection for /bin/ls.
total 11
dr-xr-xr-x 2 root    system    512 Dec 28 12:57 docs
-r-r-r- 1 root    system   2435 Feb 8 00:26 gatekeeper.home.html
-r-r-r- 1 root    system    455 Dec 29 22:17 gatekeeper.temphome.html
lrwxr-xr-x 1 root    system     20 Feb 8 00:20 home.html -> gatekeeper.ho
me.html
dr-xr-xr-x 2 root    system    512 Feb 8 23:13 includes
dr-xr-xr-x 2 root    system    512 Feb 8 00:35 info
dr-xr-xr-x 2 root    system    512 Feb 8 00:35 orgs
dr-xr-xr-x 2 root    system    512 Dec 29 22:05 pics
dr-xr-xr-x 2 root    system    512 Dec 28 12:57 util
226 Transfer complete.
remote: hypertext
619 bytes received in 0.28 seconds (2.2 Kbytes/s)
ftp>        various files are listed
```

Calling such a procedure complex would be an understatement. FTP is fast and easy to use after you learn all the magic, of course, but the point of working with computers is that you should be able to focus on *what* you want to accomplish, not on *how* you need to accomplish it.

Compare the preceding example with the procedure for using Netscape to access the same archive directly (see Figure 1-3). Instead of typing all that information, you simply *open* location `ftp://gatekeeper.dec.com/hypertext`. In this example, `ftp` indicates what kind of service is available, the `://` part is some fancy (if mysterious) notation, and `gatekeeper.dec.com/hypertext` is the name of the computer and the directory to view. Press Enter.

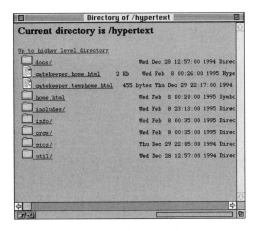

Figure 1-3: Netscape visits DEC's Gatekeeper FTP archive.

The location format (`ftp://gatekeeper.dec.com/hypertext`) is called a URL, which stands for Uniform Resource Locator.

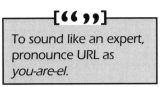

To sound like an expert, pronounce URL as *you-are-el.*

Ready to visit a directory or folder listed? Click on it, and you'll move to that spot. Ready to grab a file? Just click on the file, and Netscape automatically figures out the file type, asks what you want to call the file on your PC, and transfers it across. No fuss, no hassle.

Easy FTP isn't a unique feature of Netscape, but a capability of *all* Web browser packages, including winWeb (the browser contained on the disk in the back of this book). Figure 1-4 shows the same place (Digital's FTP site) in Mosaic.

Here's where the difference between the *paper* and the *words* becomes important: the type of service that you can connect with is what I'll call the *information transfer level,* and the actual information presented is the *content.* Some of the Web documents available on the Internet aren't actually saved and available directly within the Web itself, but are accessible directly via FTP. Figure 1-5 shows an example: the first portion of a cool home page which is accessible only with an FTP program or, of course, with your Web browser reading FTP information. The URL for the document in Figure 1-5 is `ftp://ftp.netcom.com/pub/jc/jca/homepage.html`.

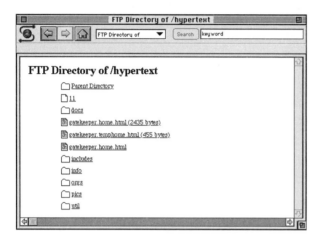

Figure 1-4: Mosaic visits DEC's Gatekeeper FTP archive.

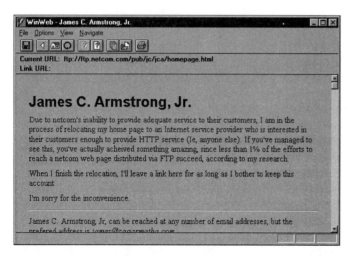

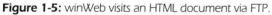

Figure 1-5: winWeb visits an HTML document via FTP.

Gopher and telnet

Web browsers also can traverse *Gopher* information space and help you *telnet* to other computers. To see how helpful those capabilities can be, consider how things were done in the days before the Web took a stab at unifying the various interfaces. Figure 1-6 shows a screen from the Windows program HGopher. The application is easy to use, but it can't help you with FTP, Web documents, or anything else.

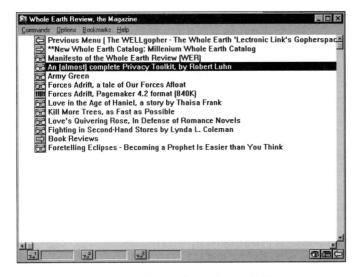

Figure 1-6: *HGopher is a limited alternative to Web browsers.*

Telnet is fairly easy to use; from your UNIX host, you simply type the word **telnet** followed by the name of the computer you want to connect to. But there's the rub: How do you remember all the computer names? The capability to be an easy, unified starting point for the different Internet services is a real selling point for a Web browser.

Figure 1-7 shows a Web page in which the links actually are pointers to different types of Internet services. Using this Web page, you don't have to remember the name of the remote computer or how to get to the place.

As you learn how to design and create Web documents, you also will learn how to choose among the various services on the Net and how to use them.

Click here to continue. (Just kidding.)

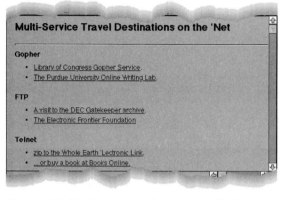

Multi-Service Travel Destinations on the 'Net

Gopher

- Library of Congress Gopher Service.
- The Purdue University Online Writing Lab.

FTP

- A visit to the DEC Gatekeeper archive.
- The Electronic Frontier Foundation

Telnet

- zip to the Whole Earth 'Lectronic Link,
- ...or buy a book at Books Online.

Figure 1-7: Multiple services from a single Web page.

In this chapter, you quickly toured some of the sites available on the Net and saw how you can use Web pointers to access more than just HTML documents. You learned that you can use Web browsers to transfer files via FTP, search Gopher sites, and jump to other machines on the Internet via Telnet. In the next chapter, I delve into the mysteries of constructing the URLs that are the heart of the Web information-linking scheme.

URLs: What They Are and How to Use Them

This chapter discusses the various types of URLs (Uniform Resource Locators)—where they came from, what they're all about, and how to make them for your own use. It includes brief discussions of FTP, Gopher, telnet and e-mail as they relate to URL construction.

In this chapter

❑ Where URLs came from
❑ What URLs are all about
❑ Various types of URLs, based on service type

Are you itching to start writing your own HTML documents and creating a world of information on the Web? Take heart — when you've mastered the concepts in this chapter, you'll be ready to start tackling the fun stuff!

Finding Information in the Flood of Data

As our society has made the transition from products to information, we have seen the rapid acceleration of an age-old problem: identifying needed resources. Finding and obtaining resources have been important themes of world history, whether it be spices, fuel, raw materials, or information.

Today, it would seem that computers should make searching *easier*. After all, aren't computers supposed to be experts at sifting through large bodies of data to find what you seek? Well, yes and no.

First, I should differentiate between data and information. *Data* is "stuff" — an all-encompassing body including every iota of digital memory and space on hard disks and backup tapes. *Information*, on the other hand, is the data that is relevant to and valuable for your specific interests. If you're interested in Beat poets of the 1960s, for example, information on other topics, such as municipal drainage systems or needlepoint, isn't informative at all but rather is clutter.

Computers have tremendously expanded the proliferation of data. As a result, separating out information from the massive flood of data is one of the fundamental challenges of the age of information. I can only imagine how much worse the situation will get in the next decade, as more and more data flows down the wires.

When considered in this vein, the Internet has a big problem. Because it has no central authority or organization, the Net's vast stores of data are not laid out in any meaningful or intuitive fashion. You are just as likely to find information on Beat poets on a machine run by a German embassy as you are to find it on a small liberal-arts school's computer in San Francisco.

URLs to the Rescue

CERN is a high-energy physics research facility in Switzerland that created the underlying technology of the World Wide Web. When Tim Berners-Lee and his team at CERN began to create a common mechanism for uniquely identifying information in dataspace, they realized the need for a scheme that would neatly encapsulate the various parts and that could be extended to include a wide variety of Internet services. The result was the URL.

To state the case succinctly, a URL (Uniform Resource Locator) is a unique descriptor that can identify any document (plain or hypertext), graphic, Gopher menu or item, Usenet article, computer, or even an archive of files anywhere on the Internet or your machine. That's what makes URLs so tremendously valuable, although their format seems a bit puzzling and cryptic at first.

The name *URL* can be something of a misnomer. Many times, jotting down URLs as you surf the Web only helps you find resources the *second* time, serving as a sort of memo service for your Internet travels. Resource location — finding information for the *first* time on the Internet and the World Wide Web — is a problem I explore later in this book. For now, think of URLs as "business cards" for specific resources on the network.

How to Read a URL

On the plus side, the format for specifying a URL is consistent throughout the many services that the URL encompasses, including Usenet news, Gopher, Web HTML documents, and FTP archives. As a general rule, a URL is composed of the following elements:

```
service  ://    host name: port    /      directory-path
```

Not all of these components appear in each URL, as you will see when you learn about the different types of URLs for different services. But the preceding example is a good general guide.

Consider the following example:

```
http://www.mecklerweb.com/home.html
```

In this example, the service is identified as `http`. (HTTP stands for *HyperText Transport Protocol*, the method by which Web documents are transferred across the Internet.) By using `http:`, you indicate to the *client* program — the program, such as Mosaic, winWeb, MacWeb, or Netscape, which you use on your computer to browse the Web — that you'll be connecting to a Web document. The host computer that offers the information you seek is `www.mecklerweb.com`. The `com` (called the *zone*) tells you that the site is a commercial site, `mecklerweb` is the *domain* or *host*, and `www` is the name of the Web server, a particular computer. Usually, as is the case here, you don't have to specify a *port* (ports are sort of like "channels" on TV) because most servers use standard, default port numbers. `home.html` is the file to open.

The following URL is a slightly more complex example:

```
ftp://ftp.cts.com/pub/wallst
```

The URL identifies a file archive for the firm Wall Street Direct (I just happen to know this). You can see that the URL points to an archive by its service identifier (ftp, which stands for *File Transport Protocol*, the way files are copied over the Net). The server and host in question is ftp.cts.com. Notice that this URL specifies that upon connecting to the FTP server, the browser program should change to the /pub/wallst directory and display the files therein.

Here's one more example:

```
news:alt.internet.services
```

The preceding URL enables a browser to read the Usenet newsgroup alt.internet.services, and you will notice that it is quite different from the other URL examples. For one thing, it doesn't specify a host. When you set up your browser program (the details differ from browser to browser), you indicate in a preferences or configuration file which host you can use to access Usenet. Usually, the host is the news server at your Internet provider. As a result, no slashes are required in the URL because the browser already has that information. URLs for news resources therefore boil down to simply the service and newsgroup name.

You can specify a variety of Internet information-publishing services with Uniform Resource Locators. The actual meanings of the URL components differ subtly, depending on which type of service is being specified. In the following sections, I examine URLs for each service in more detail.

FTP via URL

If you are familiar with the historical roots of the Internet and its predecessor networks (notably ARPANET), you already know that one of the earliest uses of the system was to transfer files quickly between hosts at different sites. The standard mechanism for accomplishing file transfers was and still is FTP. But as computers have acquired friendlier interfaces, FTP has remained in the Stone Age. Many users still use clunky command-line interfaces for this vital function.

FTP via a Web browser is much nicer.

Anonymous FTP

Millions of files are accessible throughout the Net via FTP. At a majority of hosts, you don't even need an account to download the files you seek. That's because a standard Net practice called *anonymous FTP* enables any user to log in to an FTP host using the name *anonymous*. If asked for a password, you type in your e-mail address. Among other uses, you can use anonymous FTP to acquire new programs for your computer.

FTP was one of the first services addressed in the URL specification developed at CERN. An FTP URL takes the following form:

```
ftp://host/directory-path
```

The URL `ftp://gatekeeper.dec.com/pub`, for example, uniquely specifies the `pub` directory of files available via FTP at the host `gatekeeper` at Digital Equipment Corporation.

In fact, the URL `ftp://gatekeeper.dec.com/pub` specifies more, if only by omission: by not including a username and password, the URL tells you that the site is accessible by anonymous FTP.

Non-anonymous FTP

Although most Web browser FTP-ing is done anonymously, FTP URLs *can* include the username and password for a specific account. If I had the account *coolweb* on DEC's machine, and the password were *xyzxyz,* I could modify the URL to allow other people to connect to that account, as in the following example:

```
ftp://coolweb:xyzxyz@gatekeeper.dec.com/pub
```

Ports

Things can get even more complex when you start dealing with ports. FTP, like other programs on Internet servers, may be listening to ports other than the default port for its type of service.

Let me explain: Imagine that each computer on the Internet is like a TV station/TV set: it doesn't broadcast and receive all data across all possible frequencies; it aims specific types of data, formatted in proscribed manners, at individual frequencies or channels. On the Internet, those "channels" are called *ports*. If you want to watch your local ABC affiliate, for example, you may know that the station comes in on Channel 7 and not on Channel 4. By the same token, if you want to connect to the mail server on a specific computer, you may know that the server has a *default port* of 25. Some sites, however, opt to change these default port numbers (don't ask why). In such cases, you need to identify the special port within the URL.

What if a site decides to offer anonymous FTP for public use but uses port 494 instead of the default FTP port? Then you have to specify that channel number in the URL, as in the following example:

```
ftp://gatekeeper.dec.com:494/pub
```

The preceding URL makes a browser connect to channel 494, look for the FTP server, and then move to the pub directory therein.

If you want to use your own account and password simultaneously, simply put together the URL that contains all the necessary information, as follows:

```
ftp://coolweb:xyzxyz@gatekeeper.dec.com:494/pub
```

Fortunately, you're unlikely to see anything so complex with an FTP URL. In most cases, you'll have the URL so you can look at it and see its components, even though it may be somewhat intimidating.

Using FTP URLs

The most valuable thing about FTP URLs is that, if you specify a directory, most Web browsers list the files in that directory, and with a double-click you can either transfer the files you want or move into other directories to continue browsing. If you specify a file within the URL, the browser connects to the server and transfers the file directly to your computer.

The following example is a URL containing all the information you need to obtain a copy of the HTTP specification document, should you for some strange reason want to read this highly complex and lengthy technical description of the transport protocol:

> ―**[" "]**―
>
> If you want to describe a URL to someone, you could say, "Connect via FTP on port 494 to system `gatekeeper.dec.com`, log in as *coolweb* with password *xyzxyz*, and then change to the `pub` directory."

```
ftp://ftp.w3.org/pub/www/doc/http-spec.txt
```

Are you curious about what else is in that directory? To find out, use the same URL except omit the actual file name at the end, as in

```
ftp://ftp.w3.org/pub/www/doc/
```

Gopher via URL

URLs for FTP archives are rather tricky, but they're nothing compared to Gopher URLs. If you've used the Gopher Internet service at all, you already know that it's a nicely designed heiarchical menu system for browsing file and text archives, sort of like a massively extended file system. Gopher service design involves a simple dialogue between the Gopher client (on your PC) and the Gopher server (somewhere on the Net).

Be aware, however, that the descriptions of menu items in Gopher don't necessarily correspond to the Gopher internal names for the items.

Climbing a Gopher tree

I'll give you an example. By default, specifying a host within Gopher connects you to the top level of the Gopher menu, sometimes called a *tree,* on that host. (It's confusing — think of the tree as being upside-down.) For the most part, Gopher menu items can be files or other menus. Choosing items from the Gopher menu either moves you down the tree or retrieves the items.

If you choose the third menu item from the top level menu of the Gopher server running at `wiretap.spies.com`, for example, you get a new set of menu items, as shown in Figure 2-1. The top menu item is `Electronic Books at Wiretap`. Choosing `get info` from the Gopher client program, however, reveals that the internal Gopher identification, the actual directory for `Electronic Books at Wiretap`, is `/Books`.

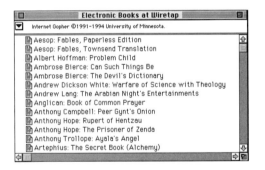

Figure 2-1: `wiretap.spies.com` with TurboGopher.

It gets stickier. Within a Gopher URL, a single-character prefix in a Gopher address identifies the Gopher item's type. For example, `0` denotes files, and `1` denotes directories (folders). Therefore, to fully specify the directory shown as item 2 in Figure 2-1, you must preface the Gopher directory in the URL with `1/`, as follows:

```
1/Books
```

How does the numerical prefix translate into a URL? Quite simply: it's tacked onto the end of the URL in the same way that the directory path and filename information were included with the FTP URL, to wit:

```
gopher://wiretap.spies.com/1/Books
```

■ ■

In case the use of uppercase and lowercase characters hasn't already tipped you off, remember that URLs are case-sensitive. Type them *exactly* as you see them.

Translating spaces in URLs

URLs have a couple of subtle limitations, the most important of which is the fact that *a URL cannot contain spaces.*

■ ■

Repeat: *URLs cannot contain spaces.*

This "no spaces" limitation caused me much consternation and some lengthy debugging sessions when I started working with Web servers. The other limitation, of course, is that they're case-sensitive even on machines that are otherwise case insensitive for filenames.

If you have a space in a Gopher address or menu name, for example, you have to translate each space into a special character that is understood to represent a space within a URL. You can't use the underscore character (_), however. That character may be used to mean something else in some systems, and automatically translating it into a space doubtless would break many things. You wouldn't want to do that.

Instead, the URL specification allows any character to be specified as — ready for this? — *a hexadecimal equivalent prefaced by a percent sign (%).* To use test server in a URL, for example, replace the space with its hexadecimal equivalent (20), resulting in test%20server.

Hexadecimal (base 16) numbers range not from 0 to 9, as in the decimal (base 10) system, but from 0 to 15. Actually, here are the hexadecimal numerals: 0, 1, 2, 3, 4, 5, 6, 7, 8, 9, A, B, C, D, E, F.

To compute the decimal equivalent of a hexadecimal number, multiply each number by the base raised to the appropriate power. Hex 20 therefore would be $2 * 16^1 + 0 * 16^0$, or 32 decimal. (Don't worry if this doesn't make sense; you'll probably never need to figure this out. Just remember to check Table 2-1 for the most common hex equivalents.)

Table 2-1 shows the special URL forms of some common characters that you may encounter while building URL specifications. Notice especially that you also need to codify any use of the percent sign *itself* so the Web browser program doesn't get confused. Almost perverse, eh?

Table 2-1: URL Coding for Common Characters		
Character	**Hex Value**	**Equivalent URL Coding**
Space	20	%20
Tab	09	%09
Enter	10	%0A
Line feed	0D	%0D
Percent	25	%25

Real-life Gopher URLs

Now that you've learned more than you ever wanted to know about Gophers and URLs, you're ready to look at some actual Gopher URLs! The good news is that the majority of Gopher URLs don't look much different from their FTP cousins, as the following example shows:

```
gopher://owl.trc.purdue.edu/
```

The preceding example is the simplest possible Gopher URL. The URL specifies the Gopher service (gopher://) and the name of the server system (owl.trc.purdue.edu/). In this case, the system is a server at Purdue University (my alma mater).

Here is another example:

```
gopher://press-gopher.uchicago.edu:70/1
```

That URL specifies the main information Gopher for the University of Chicago Press. Instead of using the default Gopher port, though, the site opted for port 70 (who knows why?). After the port, the URL indicates that the first thing the user will see is a directory, specified in a Gopher URL by inserting /1. When no *specific* directory is indicated in the URL, the preceding URL actually accomplishes exactly the same thing as the slightly simpler

```
gopher://press-gopher.uchicago.edu:70/
```

Here is a slightly longer example:

```
gopher://boombox.micro.umn.edu/0/gopher/Macintosh-TurboGopher/helper-
applications/Anarchie-140.sit
```

That URL loads an executable file (Anarchie) that is available through the Gopher server. Anarchie, for those on a Macintosh, is a fabulous shareware program that lets you easily access the Archie FTP database system and then actually grabs the files for you. Think of Archie as an intelligent assistant who finds and obtains copies of any software or files you want on the Internet.

Electronic Mail via URL

URLs for e-mail are quite simple, fortunately, and require minimal explanation. You can specify any e-mail address as a URL simply by prefacing the snippet mailto: as the service name, as in the following example:

```
mailto:taylor@netcom.com
```

Again, make sure that you don't use spaces in the URL.

Note that you can *send* e-mail in a URL but you cannot *retrieve* it.

Some browsers, such as Mosaic, launch a separate e-mail program to handle e-mail services. Others, such as Netscape, handle e-mail directly. A box pops up which allows you to compose and send mail (albeit with little control of the final content when compared to a full-blown electronic mail package like Eudora).

Telnet via URL

Transferring files through FTP is unquestionably valuable (hence its status as one of the original Internet services). Another capability that caused Internet use to explode is *telnet*. Telnet gives everyone on the Net the ability to log in to other computers on the Net, just as though they were connected to that machine directly. Not all Internet computers support telnet, but many do.

Telnet, you will be glad to know, is easy to specify in URLs: you simply specify the service and the host to which you want to connect. For example, to log in to the Massachusetts Institute of Technology's (MIT's) media laboratory, use the following URL:

```
telnet://media.mit.edu/
```

When you use telnet URLs, your Web browser program actually tries to launch a separate, external telnet program to negotiate the telnet connection, which means that nothing happens unless you've already installed and configured a separate telnet program (such as NCSA Telnet). Mosaic, Netscape, winWeb, MacWeb, and similar programs aren't designed to allow you to directly interact with the remote computer from within the browser.

Usenet News via URL

Working with Usenet news is somewhat tricky because you must find an existing server that will allow you access. Many systems don't give you that access, even if you pay for an account on the system. (A list of *public* Usenet hosts — which means hosts that attempt to provide news free of charge to all comers — is available on the Net, but in my experience, only about 5 percent of them actually allow you to connect.)

> To see the list of public Usenet sites for yourself, visit the URL `http://www.phoenix.net/config/news.html`.

If you already have access to a server that offers access to Net news, you should be able to configure your browser to access it. Alternatively, check your account settings for an `NNTPSERVER`, a computer that can usually be used to access news from your Web browser too.

Building a news URL is a straightforward process. Simply type **news:** followed by the exact name of the newsgroup. No slashes are needed (or allowed), and there's not yet a standard approach for specifying individual articles. Here are a couple of examples:

```
news:news.answers
news:comp.sys.ibm-pc.announce
```

The Heart of the Web: HTTP URLs

Although all the services listed earlier in this chapter are valuable and interesting when used via a Web browser, the capability to connect with other Web servers via HTTP (HyperText Transfer Protocol) is what *really* makes the Web revolutionary.

The general format for HTTP references is the same as in the FTP references earlier in this chapter. Following is a typical HTTP URL:

```
http://www.halcyon.com/normg/snews.html
```

That particular URL is for the *Seattle Hometown News*. You can see the secret: the URL lives within the directory of a user called `normg`. The format of the preceding URL should be quite familiar to you by this point: the service name, a colon, the double slash, the host name, a slash, some specific options (in this case, the directory `normg`), and the name of a specific file with the Web standard `html` filename extension to denote an HTML markup file.

If you're on a PC running Windows, you already know that it's unable to cope with four-letter filename suffixes. Windows simply chops off the fourth character in the extension, making it `.htm` instead. In this book I use the more proper `.html` extension.

As it turns out, many times you don't even need to specify a filename if you'd rather not do so. Following is another example of a URL, this time for the *Palo Alto Weekly* in Palo Alto, California:

```
http://www.service.com/paw/
```

Note that the URL contains a default directory (`paw`). But because the URL doesn't specify a specific filename, the Web program is savvy enough to choose the default file — probably `default.html`, as configured on each server. If your system doesn't recognize `default.html` then try `index.html` or `Welcome.html`, or ask your administrator for the secret filename!

If the HTTP server is on a nonstandard port, of course, that fact can be specified, as follows:

```
http://bookweb.cwis.uci.edu:8042/
```

The preceding URL is for the University of California at Irvine bookstore. Instead of using the default port for an HTTP server, the site opted for port 8042. If you wanted to create a URL that contained both the port and a specific filename, you could do so, as in the following example:

```
http://bookweb.cwis.uci.edu:8042/Anime/AMG/intro.html
```

Theoretically, you can specify an unlimited number of different kinds of URL types (although you probably don't want to know that at this point!). The vast majority of the URLs that you'll see, however, are in the `http`, `ftp`, `telnet`, `gopher`, `mailto`, and `news` formats, as demonstrated in this chapter.

• •

A great deal of information is jammed into this chapter, so don't be too nervous if you feel a teeny bit lost. The main point of this chapter is to give you a passing familiarity with what URLs are, how they're built, and how different types of services require different URL formats. In a few chapters, you learn how to tie URLs into your own Web documents; after that, the material in this chapter doubtless will crystallize and make much more sense. The next chapter begins the fun part of this book (indeed, the heart of the book): how to write cool Web documents!

Basic HTML

This chapter covers the basics of creating an HTML document, including head and body information, meaningful page titles, paragraph and section head marks, horizontal rules, and other, miscellaneous layout information and data.

In this chapter

- ❑ Basics of HTML layout
- ❑ Breaking at lines and paragraphs
- ❑ Breaking your document into sections
- ❑ Headers and footers
- ❑ Defining section heads
- ❑ Horizontal rules to aid visual organization

OK — it's time to get going and learn HTML! In this chapter, you'll go from 0 to 60 in no time flat, and by the end of it, you'll be able to create attractive Web pages.

Basics of HTML Layout

What is HTML? At its most fundamental, HTML (*HyperText Markup Language*) is a set of special codes that you embed in text to add formatting and linking information. HTML is based on SGML (*Standardized General Markup Language*). By convention, all HTML information begins with an open angle bracket (<) and ends with a close angle bracket (>). For example, <HTML>. That *tag* — or *HTML tag*, as it's also known — tells an HTML *interpreter* (browser) that the document is written and marked up in standard HTML. An example of an HTML interpreter would be winWeb, the World Wide Web browser program included on the disk in the back of this book.

HTML, as does any other markup language, inherits some problems. Suppose, for example, that you want to have the word *<HTML>* — including angle brackets — in a document. You need some way to prevent that word from being interpreted as an HTML tag. Later in this book, you'll learn how to include such tricky information within your documents. For now, keep an eye open for this kind of problem as you read along.

HTML and browsers

What happens if a program that interprets HTML, such as winWeb, reads a file that doesn't contain any HTML tags? Suppose that you recently created the file `not-yet.html` but haven't had a chance to add HTML tags. Your file looks something like this:

```
Dave's Desk
West Lafayette, Indiana
19 February, 1995

Dear Reader,

    Thank you for connecting to my Web server, but I
regret to tell you
that things aren't up and running yet!
They will be _soon_, but they aren't today.

                Sincerely,

                Dave Taylor
```

Looks reasonable, although some of the lines seem to be shorter than you're used to when you read such notes. Figure 3-1 shows what the file look like when it's read into the winWeb browser.

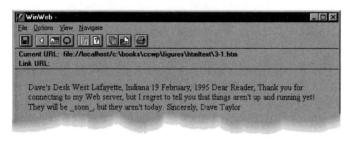

Figure 3-1: The file not-yet.html, without any HTML, in winWeb.

Figure 3-1 is clearly not at all what you wanted and probably would be quite puzzling to a reader. Notice also that, although placing an underscore before and after a word is a clue in some systems that the word should be underlined (_soon_), that's *not* part of HTML, so the underscores are left untouched, whether or not they make sense to the viewer.

["]
HTML is pronounced by saying each letter. Don't say "hittamul."

What the document shown in Figure 3-1 needs are some HTML tags — some information that Web browser programs can use to lay out and format the information therein. The implied formatting information contained in not-yet.html works for humans visually, but Web browsers would ignore it because it's not in HTML. In other words, to you or me, seeing a tab as the first character of a sentence is a good clue that the sentence is the beginning of a new paragraph, but as you can clearly see in Figure 3-1, that just isn't the case with World Wide Web browsers.

The example shown in Figure 3-1 may seem a little silly right now. But as you work with HTML, I'm sure you'll discover that when you think you set up a document in a certain way, from time to time you'll find that the document looks dramatically different from within a Web browser than you expected.

Always test your HTML documents by viewing them through one or more Web browser programs to ensure that everything looks correct.

If you open it, close it

Although many HTML tags are stand-alone units, some are *paired,* with beginning and end tags. The beginning tag is called the *open* tag, and the end tag is called the *close* tag.

The most basic of all tags is the one shown earlier: <HTML>, which indicates that the information which follows it is written in HTML. The <HTML> tag is a paired tag, however, so you need to add a close tag at the end of the document, which is the same as the open tag with the addition of a slash: </HTML>. By the same token, if you begin an italics phrase with <I> (the italics tag) you must end it with </I>. Everything between the open and close tags receives the particular attribute of that tag (the procedure of surrounding what you want to format is called *section-block notation*).

If you get confused and specify, for example, a backslash instead of a slash, as in <\HTML>, or some other variant, the browser program doesn't understand and simply ignores the close tag, and the attributes in the open tag continue past the point where you meant them to stop. In the case of the <HTML> tag, because </HTML> should appear at the end of the document, the problem probably isn't significant because there would be nothing after it to mess up. But some systems on the Net are very picky and can show some peculiar results for HTML tags that aren't closed.

> **tip**
>
> *Certainly, remembering to close any tags that you open is a good habit.*

What do you think would happen if you included quotation marks around the tags — for example, if you used "<HTML>" at the beginning of your document rather than <HTML>? If you guessed that the entire "<HTML>" including the pairs of quotes would be displayed, you're right. Let me again emphasize that the Web browsers are very simple-minded in their interpretation of HTML. Anything that varies from the specific characters in the HTML language specification results in a layout other than the one you want.

Breaking at Paragraphs and Lines

The most important markup tags you will learn — and probably the tags that you'll use most often — specify that you want a *paragraph break* or a *line break*. Several variants of these tags exist. But you can create readable and useful Web documents by using only the two tags <P> and <BR>.

To specify that you want a paragraph break, use the tag <P>. (The tag is mnemonic: *P* for *paragraph*.) The following example adds some <P> tags to the not-yet.html file seen in Figure 3-1 and also wraps the file in the <HTML> and </HTML> tags:

```
<HTML>
Dave's Desk
West Lafayette, Indiana
19 February, 1995
<P>
Dear Reader,
<P>
   Thank you for connecting to my Web server, but I
regret to tell you
that things aren't up and running yet!
They will be _soon_, but they aren't today.
<P>
                  Sincerely,
<P>
                  Dave Taylor
</HTML>
```

Figure 3-2 shows what the preceding HTML text looks like in a browser.

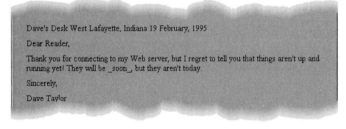

Dave's Desk West Lafayette, Indiana 19 February, 1995

Dear Reader,

Thank you for connecting to my Web server, but I regret to tell you that things aren't up and running yet! They will be _soon_, but they aren't today.

Sincerely,

Dave Taylor

Figure 3-2: Paragraph breaks in not-yet.html.

Figure 3-2's version of the file is a huge improvement over Figure 3-1's, but some problems still exist, not the least of which is the fact that the first few lines don't look right. In their zeal to organize the text neatly, Web browsers, by default, fill as many words into each line as they can manage. Filling the lines is OK for the main paragraph of the file, but the first few lines would be closer to what you want if you indicated that the browser should break the line between items, rather than fill it all in.

The way to break lines in HTML is to use the *break* tag: <BR>. Like any tag, the break tag can appear anywhere in the text, including at the end of the line you want to break. Following is the HTML file when the break tag is used:

```
<HTML>
Dave's Desk<BR>
West Lafayette, Indiana<BR>
19 February, 1995<BR>
<P>
Dear Reader, <BR>
<P>
    Thank you for connecting to my Web server, but I
regret to tell you
that things aren't up and running yet!
They will be _soon_, but they aren't today.
<P>
                    Sincerely, <BR>
<P>
                    Dave Taylor<BR>
</HTML>
```

tip From a stylistic perspective, you should try to have a consistent scheme for your tags, particularly because you may have to go into fairly complex files and figure out what's wrong. As a result, I suggest that you place all line breaks at the end of text lines and all paragraph marks in lines of their own. This book uses that style throughout.

Figure 3-3 shows the output of the not-yet.html file when <BR> is used.

Dave's Desk
West Lafayette, Indiana
19 February, 1995

Dear Reader,

Thank you for connecting to my Web server, but I regret to tell you that things aren't up and running yet! They will be _soon_, but they aren't today.

Sincerely,

Dave Taylor

Figure 3-3: The file not-yet.html with <P> and <BR> tags.

One remaining problem with the layout is the fact that the signature information is intended to be shifted to the right a few inches, as in a standard business note, but in the browser it's still left at the left edge of the document.

To remedy the problem, you can use the *preformatted information* tag: <PRE>. The <PRE> tag is also a paired tag, so it works across as many lines as needed, without any fuss, and must end with </PRE>. The following example changes the last few lines of the not-yet.html file to reflect the use of this tag:

```
<HTML>
Dave's Desk<BR>
West Lafayette, Indiana<BR>
19 February, 1995<BR>
<P>
Dear Reader, <BR>
<P>
   Thank you for connecting to my Web server, but I
regret to tell you
that things aren't up and running yet!
They will be _soon_, but they aren't today.
<PRE>
                    Sincerely,


                    Dave Taylor

</PRE>
</HTML>
```

After adding the <PRE> tags, you achieve the desired formatting, but now another problem has cropped up: the text in the preformatted block (the stuff between <PRE> and </PRE>) appears in a different, monospace typeface! You can see the difference in Figure 3-4 if you look closely.

note

Typefaces refer to a particular style of letters in a variety of sizes. A *font*, by contrast, is a typeface in a specific size and style. Helvetica is a type-face, but 12-point Helvetica italic is a font.

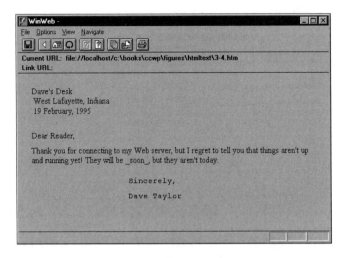

Figure 3-4: Format is correct, but typeface is new.

The reason winWeb changed the typeface in Figure 3-4 is because the browser assumed that the text to be preserved was a code listing or other technical information. That's just part of the <PRE> tag. So, it worked, sort of, but it's not quite what you wanted. (You can use <PRE> to your advantage in other situations, however, as you'll see later in this chapter.) For now, just leave the stuff at the left edge of the screen.

Breaking Your Document into Sections

If you take a close look at HTML, you see that it's divided into two sections: what I call the *stationery* section (the information that would be printed on the pad if the file were a physical note) and the body of the message itself. Think of the information you typically find at the top of a memo:

```
M E M O R A N D U M
To:                  Date:
From:                Subject:
```

Those are the most common items of information at the beginning of a memo, and then there's usually a *rule* (a line) followed by blank space in which you write the actual content of the memo.

Similarly, for the sake of organization, HTML files commonly are broken into two sections: the *head* (or *header*) that contains the introductory page-formatting information, and the *body*. You use the paired tags `<HEAD>` `</HEAD>` and `<BODY>` `</BODY>` to surround each section. The following example shows how the `not-yet.html` file looks when these tags are added:

```
<HTML>
<HEAD></HEAD>
<BODY>
Dave's Desk<BR>
West Lafayette, Indiana<BR>
19 February, 1995<BR>
<P>
Dear Reader,
<P>
   Thank you for connecting to my Web server, but I
regret to tell you
that things aren't up and running yet!
They will be _soon_, but they aren't today.
<P>
                  Sincerely,
<P>
                  Dave Taylor
</BODY>
</HTML>
```

The `<HEAD>` `</HEAD>` and `<BODY>` `</BODY>` formatting information doesn't add anything to the display, I admit. Also, the document doesn't contain any introductory HTML formatting information yet. If you were to view the preceding HTML text in a Web browser, it would look identical to Figure 3-3. Later, when you start learning some of the more complex parts of HTML, you'll see why section-block notation (e.g., `<HEAD></HEAD>`) can be a boon.

What do you think would happen if I fed the following information to a Web browser?

```
<HTML><HEAD></HEAD><BODY>
Dave's Desk<BR>West Lafayette, Indiana<BR>19 February, 1995<BR>
<P>Dear Reader,<P>Thank you for connecting to
my Web server, but I regret to tell you that
things aren't up and running yet!
They will be _soon_, but they aren't today.
<P>Sincerely,<P>Dave Taylor</BODY></HTML>
```

If you guessed that the screen output of the preceding example would look exactly like the carefully spaced material shown earlier, you're correct.

tip Remember that Web browsers ignore carriage returns when the document is reformatted for display. That suggests that you can save a great deal of space — and display a great deal more of your document on-screen — simply by skipping all the extra returns — *but I strongly recommend against such a strategy.* Why? In a nutshell, writing your Web documents with the markup tags in logical places makes the document easier to work with later. I've written and had to debug more than 500 HTML documents, and I can assure you that the more things are jammed together, the less sense they make a few weeks later, when you find out that you have to add some information or modify the content.

Title Your Page

One of the subtle (but quite simple) things you can do to make your Web page quite cool is give it a good title with the <TITLE> tag. The title usually appears at the top of the window displayed on the user's computer. Go back and look at the information in the top of header of Figure 3-4: that's the entire filename on my machine, which is clunky to read and not very helpful!

The <TITLE> tag allows you to define the exact title you want in the document. It is a paired tag and appears within the <HEAD> </HEAD> block of information, as follows:

```
<HEAD>
<TITLE>This is the title</TITLE>
</HEAD>
```

For the document we've been developing in this chapter, `not-yet.html`, a nice title would be one that reinforces the message in the file itself, as in the following example:

```
<HTML>
<HEAD>
<TITLE>Not Yet Ready for Prime Time!</TITLE>
</HEAD>
```

Figure 3-5 shows how the new title text would look within the winWeb browser. Notice particularly the change in the top window border (also known as the title bar).

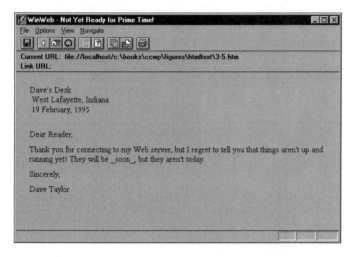

Figure 3-5: TITLE produces an attractive window frame.

The `<TITLE>` tag has one limitation: Some Web browsers don't display titled windows, so the `<TITLE>` information isn't displayed for folks using those browsers. On the other hand, the text in `<TITLE>` is also used as the link info when a user saves a Web document into a *bookmark* or *hotlist* (compiled URLs for sites you've visited and want to remember). So, a meaningful `<TITLE>` for each page you create can be very helpful to your readers.

Common Footer Material

Just as you commonly see certain information, such as the title, in the header of a Web document, certain other information is commonly placed at the foot of the document. On the Web, you usually find copyright information and contact data for the creator of the page at the bottom of documents.

The tag used for such contact info is <ADDRESS>. It's a paired tag (<ADDRESS> *address information* </ADDRESS>). The following example shows this tag added to the not-yet.html document:

```
<HTML>
<HEAD>
<TITLE>Not Yet Ready for Prime Time!</TITLE>
</HEAD>
<BODY>
Dave's Desk<BR>
West Lafayette, Indiana<BR>
19 February, 1995<BR>
<P>
Dear Reader,
<P>
Thank you for connecting to my Web server, but I
regret to tell you
that things aren't up and running yet!
They will be _soon_, but they aren't today.
<P>
                    Sincerely,
<P>
                    Dave Taylor
<ADDRESS>
Page Design by Dave Taylor (taylor@netcom.com)
</ADDRESS>
</BODY>
</HTML>
```

Do you *have* to use the <ADDRESS> tag? Nope. Like various other items that appear in HTML pages, it can be used or skipped. (In Web pages that I create, I tend not to include address information, but many people like to have that information at the bottom of pages.) That's why I call tags like <ADDRESS> *quasi-standard* — it's useful, but not always present. As you can see in Figure 3-6, the address stuff is presented in italics, which is quite attractive for certain Web pages.

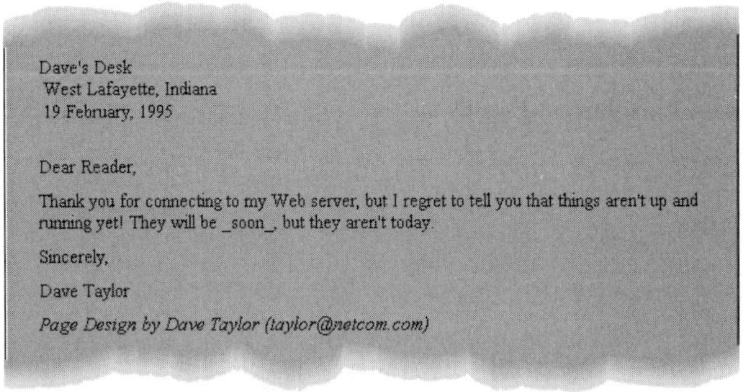

Dave's Desk
West Lafayette, Indiana
19 February, 1995

Dear Reader,

Thank you for connecting to my Web server, but I regret to tell you that things aren't up and running yet! They will be _soon_, but they aren't today.

Sincerely,

Dave Taylor

Page Design by Dave Taylor (taylor@netcom.com)

Figure 3-6: <HTML> plus <ADDRESS> information.

Defining Section Heads

The formatting information discussed so far in this chapter enables you to create attractive text. But what if your Web page should be broken into *sections* or even *subsections*? The various levels of *header-format* tags handle that situation.

Each header-format level has an open and close tag. The highest-level header-format tag is H1; the lowest (the smallest and least important subsection) is H6. To specify a top-level header, use <H1>First Header</H1>.

Header-format tags would be best illustrated in a different HTML page than not-yet.html, because it doesn't need headers and is already attractive. The following is the beginning of a table of contents or outline for an imaginary Web site:

```
<HTML>
<HEAD>
<TITLE>The Cool Web Movie Database</TITLE>
</HEAD>
<BODY>
Welcome to the Cool Web Movie Database. So far, we offer information on
the many brilliant films of David Lean; soon, many more will be online.
<H1>The Early Years</H1>
<H2>In Which We Serve (1942)</H2>
<H2>This Happy Breed (1944)</H2>
<H1>Films with Sam Spiegel Productions</H1>
<H2>The Bridge on the River Kwai (1957)</H2>
<H2>Lawrence of Arabia (1962)</H2>
<H1>The Later Years</H1>
<H2>Doctor Zhivago (1965)</H2>
<H2>Ryan's Daughter (1970)</H2>
<ADDRESS>
This information maintained by Dave Taylor
</ADDRESS>
</BODY>
</HTML>
```

Figure 3-7 shows how the preceding text appears in a Web browser.

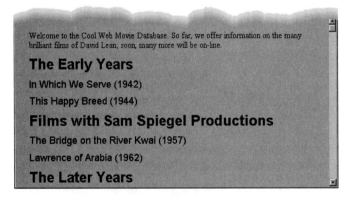

Figure 3-7: David Lean movies, outline form.

Most Web pages that you design probably won't have *quite* as many headers as the example in Figure 3-7.

The following example adds a little more information about some of the films to show the value of different headers:

```
<H1>The Early Years</H1>
<H2>In Which We Serve (1942)</H2>
Co-directed and produced by Noel Coward, this film also starred
Noel Coward as Captain Kinross and Celia Johnson as Mrs. Kinross.
<H2>This Happy Breed (1944)</H2>
Based on the play by Noel Coward, this film starred Robert Newton and
again featured Celia Johnson.
<H1>Films with Sam Spiegel Productions</H1>
<H2>The Bridge on the River Kwai (1957)</H2>
Produced by Sam Spiegel, this film was the first of the Lean blockbuster
movies and featured a young Alec Guinness, William Holden, and a
brilliant performance from Sessue Hayakawa.
<H2>Lawrence of Arabia (1962)</H2>
One of my personal all-time favorite movies, this epic adventure
really established Lean as the creator of sweeping panoramas.
```

When the preceding example is viewed in a browser, the different headers appear in different size type, and information that is *not* part of the header appears in a roman (nonbold) typeface (see Figure 3-8).

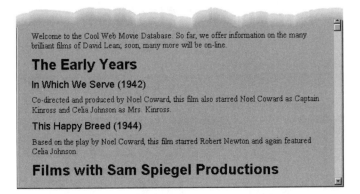

Figure 3-8: Movie information with some text — nice, eh?

One thing to remember about HTML is that the actual fonts, sizes, and layout of the final presentation can be altered by users based on the preferences they can set in their browsers. I contend, however, that precious few people actually alter the preference settings, so if your page looks good with the default values, you should be OK. If the default values look a little weird, as may well be the case with winWeb in particular, by all means experiment with the settings.

The Horizontal Rule

A very useful tag for readers is the *horizontal rule* tag: <HR>. Dropped anywhere in a Web document, it produces a skinny line across the page. The following example shows the movie-information page with the <HR> tag added:

```
<HR>
<H1>The Early Years</H1>
<H2>In Which We Serve (1942)</H2>
Co-directed and produced by Noel Coward, this film also starred
Noel Coward as Captain Kinross and Celia Johnson as Mrs. Kinross.
<H2>This Happy Breed (1944)</H2>
Based on the play by Noel Coward, this film starred Robert Newton and
again featured Celia Johnson.
<HR>
<H1>Films with Sam Spiegel Productions</H1>
<H2>The Bridge on the River Kwai (1957)</H2>
Produced by Sam Spiegel, this was the first of the Lean blockbuster
movies and featured a young Alec Guinness, William Holden, and a
brilliant performance from Sessue Hayakawa.
```

You *can* overuse the horizontal rule, as well as any other formatting and design element, in a Web document. Used judiciously, though, the <HR> tag is tremendously helpful in creating cool pages. Figure 3-9 shows the browser view:

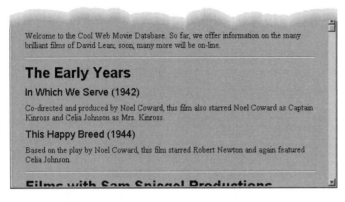

Figure 3-9: Movie database with horizontal rules.

Table 3-1 contains a summary of the HTML tags covered in this chapter.

Table 3-1	Summary of Tags in This Chapter	
HTML Tag	**Close Tag**	**Meaning**
<ADDRESS>	</ADDRESS>	Address and creator information
<BODY>	</BODY>	Body of the HTML page
 	none	Line break
<HEAD>	</HEAD>	HTML formatting information
<Hn>	</Hn>	Document header level ($n = 1$–6)
<HR>	*none*	Horizontal rule
<HTML>	</HTML>	Defines a Web-formatted file
<P>	*none*	Paragraph breaks
<PRE>	</PRE>	Preformatted information

● ●

A great deal of information was jammed into this chapter. You have learned most of the basics of HTML and are about ready to start creating your own Web pages. Already, you should be able to reproduce formatted information (like this chapter of this book, to pick the most immediate example) in an attractive format for users on the World Wide Web. The next chapter continues to explore HTML by explaining how to use boldface and italic formatting, add other types of emphasis to text, and make various other changes within sentences and paragraphs.

Text Styles

This chapter explores some of the nuts and bolts of text presentation and information layout.

In this chapter

- ❏ How to boldface and italicize text
- ❏ Underlining and monospace
- ❏ Other ways to emphasize words or phrases

By *text styles,* I mean specification of boldface, italics, and other changes that can be made in text. The preceding chapter showed you all the basics of HTML document layout in the proverbial fell swoop. But there's much more to creating cool Web pages.

When you were given your first box of Crayons, you probably went wild and tried to use all the colors on each illustration that you colored. Eventually, however, it dawned on you (unless you were a young Peter Max) that a *subset* of colors can be much more useful and attractive. The same holds true for the various formatting commands in HTML: You can use all the commands all over the place, but a better strategy is to use them only when they are most appropriate. Many Web pages tend to be already cluttered, and using too much italicization or boldface makes the clutter even worse.

Nevertheless, if you want to highlight certain words, phrases, titles, names, or other information, you'll learn how to do that within the hypertext markup language before you finish this chapter.

A Little History

Page design and layout have been around for thousands of years — since the beginning of writing as a form of communication. In Egyptian hieroglyphics, for example, vertical lines separate columns of glyphs to make them easier to read. Before the year 1000 A.D., scribes all over the world were using various techniques of presenting information on a page, including illumination (adding gold or silver to the ink or including other illustrations in the margins or twined around the letters), illustration, and other devices.

By the time Johann Gutenberg introduced his printing press in the 15th Century, with its revolutionary movable type supplanting etched- or engraved-plate printing, designers and artists were codifying various approaches to page design. A glance at the Gutenberg Bible foreshadows many aspects of modern text design, including italicized and boldface text.

Why am I rambling on about the history of page layout? Well, it's important to realize that italics and boldface text have commonly accepted standard meanings. You don't have to follow the rules to the letter, but if your goal is to help people breeze through your Web material and quickly find what they seek, then keeping the guidelines in mind can be quite valuable.

Bold and Italic

In the examples in Chapter 3, I mentioned that some standard computer notation for underlining doesn't work. In Figure 3-1, I included the example _soon_, hoping that when read by a browser, the word would be italicized, underlined, or otherwise presented in a manner that would emphasize it.

One of the most important characteristics of any cool document layout — on the Web or in print — is the use of different fonts and various styles to help the reader navigate the material. For example, imagine this page without any spacing, paragraph breaks, headings, italics, or boldface words; it would look boring. More important, it would be more difficult to skim the page for information or to glance at it quickly to gain a sense of what is being discussed.

I like to remember the differences by imagining that I'm reading the material to an audience. Italicized words or phrases are those that I emphasize in my speech. Words or phrases in boldface I imagine to be anchors — items that help me skim the material and find specific spots. Apply this practice to text, and you see why section headings are in bold rather than italic: headings would be harder to find if they didn't stand out. The same reasoning applies to text size; large words stand out from smaller adjacent text.

Let's dive in and see how bold and italic work in Web page design. Italic and boldface formatting require paired tags.

- ❑ The italic formatting tag is `<I>`, which is paired with `</I>`.
- ❑ The boldface formatting tag is `<B>`, and its partner is `</B>`.

Here's how a brief HTML passage looks with both bold and italics text:

```
It turns out that <B>Starbucks</B>, the popular and
fast growing coffee chain, got its name from the
coffee-loving first mate in Melville's classic
tale of pursuit and revenge <I>Moby Dick< /I >,
although few people realize it.
```

Figure 4-1 shows how the preceding information looks in a Web browser. Notice that I made a slight mistake in the coding: the name of the book, *Moby Dick*, has an open italics tag, but I incorrectly added spaces within its partner, the close italics tag. As a result, the request to end the italics passage doesn't end when the title of the book is complete. Also, if you view this exact same snippet in Mosaic or Netscape you'll find that each has a slightly different way of dealing with an error of this form. Another good reason to double check your HTML in multiple browsers!

It turns out that **Starbucks**, the popular and fast growing coffee chain, got its name from the coffee-loving first mate in Melville's classic tale of pursuit and revenge *Moby Dick, though few people realize it.*

Figure 4-1: Boldface, italics, and a mistake.

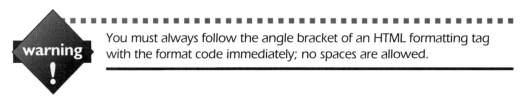

warning !

You must always follow the angle bracket of an HTML formatting tag with the format code immediately; no spaces are allowed.

Underlining and Monospace

Two other formatting options are available within Web documents: *underlining* and *monospace* (typewriter-style text):

☐ The underline formatting tag is `<U>`, which is paired with `</U>`.

☐ The monospace tag is `<TT>`, which is paired with `</TT>`.

Monospace is so named because each letter in a monospace typeface occupies exactly the same width, even if the letter itself is quite narrow. Monospace type typically looks like the product of a typewriter. `This is a monospace typeface.` Proportional typefaces are more common. The text you are reading now is a proportional typeface. Note that it varies the width of the letters for easier reading. If you take a ruler, you'll see that four occurrences of the letter *i,* for example (iiii) isn't as long as four occurrences of *m* (mmmm).

You may not want to use the `<U>` and `<TT>` tags too often, because of the possible problems. Mosaic, for example, doesn't understand the `<TT>` format, and some earlier versions of Netscape ignore `<U>` formats. Also, when you create a Web document that contains *links* to other documents, the links are displayed in a different color — usually, blue. However, to make links stand out more and to ensure that people with gray scale or black-and-white displays can recognize links, links also appear with an underscore. Which underlined words or phrases are links, and which are just underlined text? Figure 4-2 shows this underlining problem more clearly.

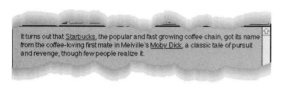

Figure 4-2: Links or underlined text?

You can't tell by looking at Figure 4-2, but the word *Starbucks* is a pointer to another document on the World Wide Web, whereas the book title, *Moby Dick*, is just an underlined word. As you can see, using underscores in Web pages can be confusing.

Monospace often is more useful than underlining, but it's not used extensively in cool Web pages either. If you want to simulate computer input or output, for example, you can display that text in monospace, as in the following:

```
Rather than typing <B><TT>DIR</TT></B> to find out what
files you have in your Unix account, you'll instead
want to type <B><TT>ls</TT></B>, as shown:
<PRE>
% <B>LS</B>
this  that          the-other
</PRE>
```

The preceding example demonstrates that the preformatted text tag <PRE> also produces text in monospace typeface, but it also preserves the original line breaks rather than filling the words into each line of text.

You can combine some HTML tags to produce exactly the output that you seek. In Figure 4-3, the terms *DIR* and *ls* appear in bold monospace text.

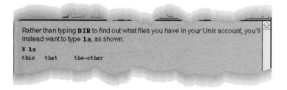

Figure 4-3: Monospace (and bold monospace) with <TT>.

note Depending on the Web browser you're using, some HTML tags can be combined, and others can't. Combining bold and italics in some cases doesn't work, but either format works when combined with <TT>.

Logical Styles

The style directives discussed up to this point are easy to understand. The HTML language also supports what are called *logical styles*. Logical styles enable readers (and their software) to define emphasis.

The most common logical styles are <EM> </EM> for emphasis and <STRONG> </STRONG> for stronger emphasis. Figure 4-4 shows an example of these tags.

I'd like to make two points during this presentation: *Things are okay* and **Things are getting better!**

Figure 4-4: Logical styles in HTML.

In the example shown in Figure 4-4, the first point (shown in italics) is specified as <EM>Things are Okay</EM>, and the second point (boldfaced) is specified as <STRONG>Things are getting better!</STRONG>.

Putting It All Together

Following is an example of a complex HTML document viewed within a Web browser. The example includes material covered in Chapters 3 and 4.

```
<HTML>
<HEAD>
<TITLE>Travels with Tintin</TITLE>
</HEAD><BODY>
<H1>Travels with Tintin</H1>
Of the various reporters with whom I've traveled around
the world, including writers for <I>UPI</I>, <I>AP</I>, and <I>Reuters
</I>, the most fascinating has clearly been <B>Tintin</B>, boy reporter
from Belgium
(<TT>tintin@belgium.gov</TT>).
<P>
Probably the most enjoyable aspect of our travels was his dog,
<B>Snowy</B>, although I don't know that our hosts would agree!
<H2>The First Trip: Nepal</H2>
After winning the Pulitzer for <I>Adventure with Red Rackham's
Treasure</I>, Tintin
told me he wanted a vacation. Remembering some
of his earlier adventures, he decided to visit Nepal. Early one Sunday, I
was sipping my tea and reading the <I>Times</I> when he rang me up,
asking whether I'd be able to take a break and come along...
</BODY>
</HTML>
```

Can you guess how the preceding text will look from a browser? Check Figure 4-5 to find out.

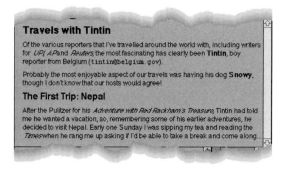

Figure 4-5: A complex and attractive document.

The document in Figure 4-5 is quite attractive, albeit with some poor spacing around the italicized acronyms in the first sentence. Fortunately some of the most recent Web browsers realize that an additional space is needed after the last italicized character, so this becomes even more readable. Also notice the automatic spacing around the <Hn> formats.

A summary of the many character formatting tags learned in this chapter is contained in Table 4-1.

Table 4-1	Summary of Tags in This Chapter	
HTML Tag	**Close Tag**	**Meaning**
<B>	</B>	Display text in bold
<I>	</I>	Display text in italic
<U>	</U>	Underline specified text
<TT>	</TT>	Monospace text
<EM>	</EM>	Logical emphasis style
<STRONG>	</STRONG>	Logical stronger emphasis

This chapter has focused on formatting characters and words. The next chapter focuses on larger formatting issues, including how to add both numbered and bullet lists to your HTML documents , and how to include glossaries or other definition lists.

Lists and Special Characters

This chapter introduces you to various types of lists for Web pages, including ordered (numbered) and unordered (bulleted) lists. It also explains how to add special and non-English characters and comments to your Web documents.

In this chapter

❑ Definition lists
❑ Ordered (numbered) and unordered (bulleted) lists
❑ Other approaches to lists
❑ Special characters in HTML documents
❑ Comments within HTML code

You'll see lots of lists on the Web. After you read this chapter, you'll be able to use the different list styles to your advantage.

Definition Lists

One of the most common elements of multipage documents is a set of definitions, references, or cross-indexes. Glossaries are classic examples; words are listed alphabetically, followed by prose definitions. In HTML, the entire section of a glossary would be contained by a *definition list,* which is contained within a pair of *definition list* tags: <DL> and </DL>. Within the pair of listings, a definition has two parts:

- ❑ Definition term (<DT>)
- ❑ Definition description (<DD>).

Here's how a definition list can be used in HTML to define some genetics terms:

```
<HTML>
<TITLE>A Quick Glossary of Genetic Terms</TITLE>
<I>Adapted from Dawkins, The Extended Phenotype</I>
<DL>
<DT>allometry
<DD>A disproportionate relationship between size of a body part and size
of the whole body.
<DT>anaphase
<DD>Phase of the cell division during which the paired chromosomes move
apart.
<DT>antigens
<DD>Foreign bodies, usually protein molecules, which provoke the
formation of antibodies.
<DT>autosome
<DD>A chromosome that is not one of the sex chromosomes.
<DT>codon
<DD>A triplet of units (nucleotides) in the genetic code, specifying the
synthesis of a single unit (amino acid) in a protein chain.
<DT>genome
<DD>The entire collection of genes possessed by one organism.
</DL>
</HTML>
```

Figure 5-1 shows how the preceding HTML code looks in a Web browser. Notice the automatic indentation and formatting.

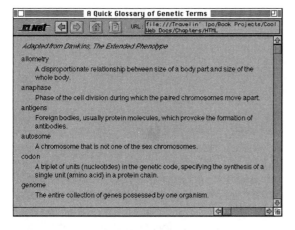

Figure 5-1: A glossary in HTML.

If you're writing a book about herbal remedies, for example, you may want to have a cross-reference of herbs for specific problems. Certain key herbs could be italicized to highlight them. The following example shows how you might want such a listing to look:

Blood Pressure

> Balm, Black Haw, *Garlic*, Hawthorn.

Bronchitis

> Angelica, *Aniseed*, *Caraway*, Grindelia

Burns

> Aloe, Chickweed, *Elder*

Obtaining the preceding format within an HTML document would require the following tag placements:

```
<DL>
<DT><B>Blood Pressure</B>
<DD>Balm, Black Haw, <I>Garlic</I>, Hawthorn.
<DT><B>Bronchitis</B>
<DD>Angelica, <I>Aniseed, Caraway</I>, Grindelia.
<DT><B>Burns</B>
<DD>Aloe, Chickweed, <I>Elder</I>.
</DL>
```

Figure 5-2 shows the result, which is, if I do say so myself, quite attractive and similar to the original design. (By this point, I hope that you can read the preceding HTML snippet and understand all the paired formatting tags. If not, you might want to nip back to Chapter 4 and study it a bit more to refresh your memory on text style formatting.)

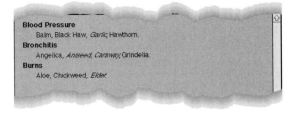

Figure 5-2: Medicinal herbs as a definition list.

The basic concept of a list is exhibited in the definition-list format: a pair of tags within which other tags have special meanings. What happens if you use `<DT>` and `<DD>` without wrapping them in a `<DL></DL>` pair? The result is identical to Figure 5-2: the default meanings of the `<DT>` and `<DD>` tags are consistent, whether they appear within a list or not. Which isn't to say that it's guaranteed to work correctly on *all* Web browsers just because it formatted correctly in the test program. Indeed, Mosaic formats a definition list wrong if it isn't surrounded by `<DL></DL>`.

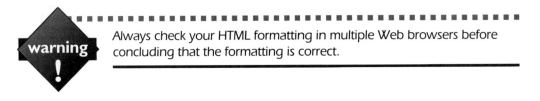

Always check your HTML formatting in multiple Web browsers before concluding that the formatting is correct.

Unordered (Bulleted) Lists

Definition lists are handy, but the type of list that you see much more often on the World Wide Web is a bulleted list, also called an *unordered list*. Unordered lists start with <UL> and close with </UL>, and each list item is denoted by the *list item* (<LI>) tag. The format is similar to that of the definition list, as the following example shows:

```
Common Herbal remedies include:
<UL>
<LI>Blood Pressure — Balm, Black Haw, <I>Garlic</I>, Hawthorn.
<LI>Bronchitis — Angelica, <I>Aniseed, Caraway</I>, Grindelia.
<LI>Burns — Aloe, Chickweed, <I>Elder</I>.
</UL>
```

The result as viewed from a browser is attractive, if somewhat confusing, as Figure 5-3 shows.

Figure 5-3: A bulleted list.

More useful is a combination of the two list types. The definition list looked very cool with the additions of boldface and indentation, but the bullets next to each item in the unordered list look slick, too. The solution is to nest lists within one another, as follows:

```
Common Herbal remedies include:
<DL>
<DT><B>Blood Pressure</B>
<UL>
<LI>Balm
<LI>Black Haw
<LI><I>Garlic</I>
```

(continued)

```
(continued)
<LI>Hawthorn.
</UL>
<DT><B>Bronchitis</B>
<UL>
<LI>Angelica
<LI><I>Aniseed</I>
<LI>Caraway
<LI>Grindelia.
</UL>
<DT><B>Burns</B>
<UL>
<LI>Aloe
<LI>Chickweed
<LI><I>Elder</I>.
</UL>
</DL>
```

Figure 5-4 shows the result of the preceding code, which is a very cool layout.

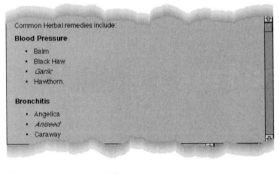

Common Herbal remedies include:

Blood Pressure

- Balm
- Black Haw
- *Garlic*
- Hawthorn.

Bronchitis

- Angelica
- *Aniseed*
- Caraway

Figure 5-4: A nested list.

The output in Figure 5-4 is what you want. But is the HTML coding behind it the best possible approach? Think about it: You define terms with `<DT>` but don't actually have any definition with `<DD>`. In this case, as it turns out, the nested list just adds to the confusion. You can achieve an identical result with the following, simpler example:

```
Common herbal remedies include:
<P>
<B>Blood Pressure</B>
<UL>
<LI>Balm
<LI>Black Haw
<LI><I>Garlic</I>
<LI>Hawthorn.
</UL>
<B>Bronchitis</B>
<UL>
<LI>Angelica
<LI><I>Aniseed</I>
<LI>Caraway
<LI>Grindelia.
</UL>
<B>Burns</B>
<UL>
<LI>Aloe
<LI>Chickweed
<LI><I>Elder</I>.
</UL>
```

The preceding example illustrates the dangers and problems in description languages such as HTML. Because you can accomplish tasks in various ways, you have to wonder: Are the most obvious methods always the *best?*

As a rule, the simpler a design is, the more likely it is to work correctly.

Ordered (Numbered) Lists

What if you want to create a list, but with numbers instead of bullet points? The adage "simpler is better" suggests the formatting in the following example:

```
<H2>Enchilada Sauce</H2>
1. Heat a large saucepan, and saute the following ingredients until soft:
<UL>
<LI>Two tablespoons virgin olive oil
<LI>Large onion, chopped
</UL>
2. Add a quart of water.<BR>
3. Sprinkle in a quarter-cup of flour.<BR>
4. Jazz it up by adding:
<UL>
<LI>Two tablespoons chili powder
<LI>Two teaspoons cumin
<LI>One teaspoon garlic powder
</UL>
5. Finally, add a teaspoon of salt, if desired.
<BR>
Whisk as sauce thickens; then simmer for 20 minutes.
```

The result is quite attractive, as Figure 5-5 shows.

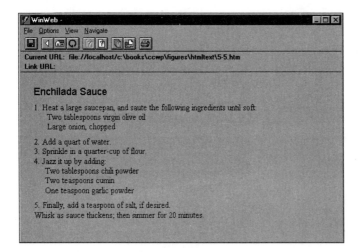

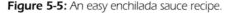

Figure 5-5: An easy enchilada sauce recipe.

Before you carry this book into the kitchen, however, I need to tell you that I got confused while I typed this recipe. The water should be added at the end, *not* in step 2.

Now what? You certainly don't want to have to renumber all the items in the numbered list. The situation calls for the cousin of the unordered list: the *ordered list* (<OL>). The list ends with the close tag </OL>. Each item in the list has a *list item* tag (<LI>). With ordered lists, unlike definition lists, you can see that it does make quite a difference whether you use the <LI> tag without an <OL></OL> list surrounding it. In an ordered list, the meaning of the tag depends on what kind of list it lies within.

Following is the way the recipe looks with my gaffe corrected and the HTML code rewritten to take advantage of the ordered-list tag:

```
<H2>Enchilada Sauce</H2>
<OL>
<LI>Heat a large saucepan, and saute the following ingredients until
soft:
<UL>
<LI>Two tablespoons virgin olive oil
<LI>Large onion, chopped
</UL>
<LI>Sprinkle in a quarter-cup of flour.
<LI>Jazz it up by adding:
<UL>
<LI>Two tablespoons chili powder
<LI>Two teaspoons cumin
<LI>One teaspoon garlic powder
</UL>
<LI>Add a quart of water.
<LI>Finally, add a teaspoon of salt, if desired.
</OL>
Whisk as sauce thickens; then simmer for 20 minutes.
```

The output (see Figure 5-6) is not only correct but is considerably more attractive as well because Web browsers automatically indent lists of this nature. As a result, the nested-list items are indented twice.

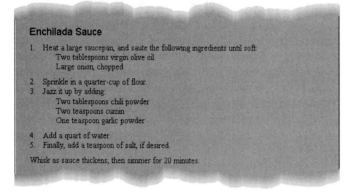

Enchilada Sauce

1. Heat a large saucepan, and saute the following ingredients until soft:
   Two tablespoons virgin olive oil
   Large onion, chopped

2. Sprinkle in a quarter-cup of flour.
3. Jazz it up by adding:
   Two tablespoons chili powder
   Two teaspoons cumin
   One teaspoon garlic powder

4. Add a quart of water.
5. Finally, add a teaspoon of salt, if desired.

Whisk as sauce thickens, then simmer for 20 minutes.

Figure 5-6: Automatic numbering and indents, too.

Other Approaches to Lists

With definition lists, ordered lists, and unordered lists, you probably can cover all your bets. One problem with these formats, however, is that the output, viewed in a Web browser, may be spaced out too much; your list may sprawl across more space than necessary. The designers of HTML tried to address the spacing problem by providing two relatively new tags: <DIR> and <MENU>.

For information that can be presented in compact form, you should use the *directory* formatting tag (<DIR>) and its partner (</DIR>). If the list items are *really* succinct (as in 20 characters or fewer), you may want to try the *menu* format (<MENU>), which produces multicolumn displays in some of the most advanced browsers.

The following example shows how the <DIR> and <MENU> formats look in a typical HTML snippet:

```
<HTML>
<HEAD>
<TITLE>Dave's On-Line Deli</TITLE>
</HEAD><BODY>
<H2>Welcome to the Virtual World of Dave's On-Line Deli!</H2>
Sandwich Choices:
<DIR>
<LI>Turkey on a croissant
```

```
<LI>Ham and cheese
<LI>Veggie Delight
</DIR>
Soups of the Day:
<MENU>
<LI>Tomato
<LI>Tomato and rice
<LI>Chicken
<LI>Lentil
<LI>Barley
<LI>Gumbo
<LI>Corn chowder
<LI>Mystery Soup
</MENU>
<I>Please order at the counter...</I>
</BODY>
</HTML>
```

What will the HTML text look like in a browser? Figure 5-7 shows that winWeb displays a simple unordered list, only without bullets next to the items (an omission that makes this page look not so cool).

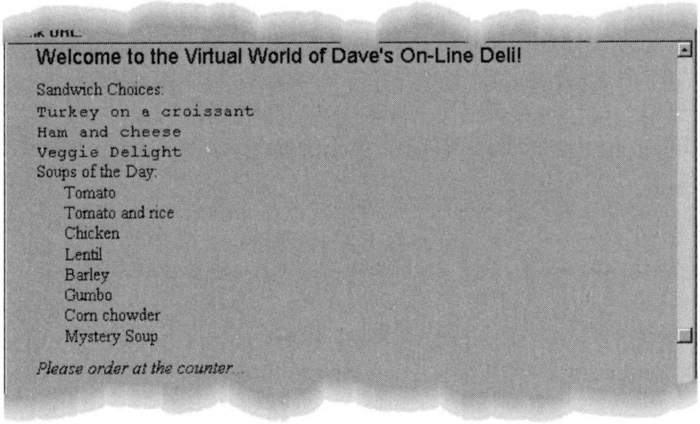

Figure 5-7: <DIR> and <MENU> items in winWeb.

If you view the same HTML document in a more sophisticated program, such as Netscape, the document is a regular unordered list with bullets (see Figure 5-8).

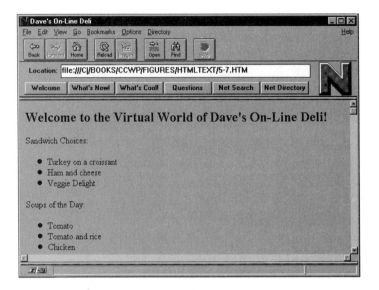

Figure 5-8: <DIR> and <MENU> items in Netscape.

To be honest, I can't find any Web browsers that correctly interpret the <MENU> and <DIR> tags. Most browsers take the formatting tag to mean that the list is just another tab-indented list, as you can see in Figures 5-7 and 5-8. Should you use these formatting options for the information in your document? It's up to you. I skip these formats in my own work. But as soon as browsers can format <MENU> items in multiple columns, I'm sure that many people will find this powerful list format to be much more interesting. I know I'll change the design of some of my Web pages.

Special Characters in HTML Documents

If you're an alert reader, you may have noticed a typographical error in the recipe shown earlier. The recipe instructed the cook to *saute* the ingredients, yet the word should have an accent (*sauté*). Languages contain a variety of special characters that you may need to use, particularly if you plan to present material in a language other than English. Not surprisingly, you can include special characters in HTML code by using special "tags," called *entities* or *entity references*.

Unlike the tags you've learned about so far, special character entities aren't neatly tucked into paired brackets (<>); instead, they always begin with an ampersand (&) and end with a semicolon (;). Most entities are somewhat mnemonic, as Table 5-1 shows.

Table 5-1	Special Characters in HTML	
Character	**HTML Code**	**Meaning**
&	&amp;	ampersand
<	&lt;	less than
>	&gt;	greater than
á	&aacute;	lowercase *a* with acute accent
à	&agrave;	lowercase *a* with grave accent
â	&acirc;	lowercase *a* with circumflex
ä	&auml;	lowercase *a* with umlaut
å	&aring;	lowercase *a* with ring
ç	&ccedil;	lowercase *c* with cedilla
ñ	&ntilde;	lowercase *n* with tilde
ø	&oslash;	lowercase *o* with slash
ß	&szlig;	lowercase sharp *s* symbol

note Not all Web browsers can display all of these characters, particularly on Windows systems. Check them on a few browsers before you use them in your own Web page layout.

To create an uppercase version of one of the characters in Table 5-1, simply make the first letter of the formatting tag uppercase. Ø, for example, produces an uppercase *O* with a slash through it, as in the word *CØPENHAGEN*. To produce a different vowel with a diacritical mark, change the first letter of that tag. The word *desvàn*, for example, is correctly specified in an HTML document as desvàn.

The following example contains some foreign-language snippets so that you can see how these formatting tags work:

```
The following are formatted with &lt;b&gt; for
boldface and &lt;i&gt; for italics.
<P>
<B>Gibt es ein Caf&eacute; in der N&auml;he? </B><BR>
<I>Is there a caf&eacute; nearby?</I><P>
<B>Je voudrais un d&icirc;ner. </B><BR>
<I>I want to eat dinner.</I><P>
<B>Y una mesa por ma&ntilde;ana, por favor.</B><BR>
<I>And a table for tomorrow, please.</I><P>
<B>Oh! C'&egrave; una specialit&agrave; locale?</B><BR>
<I>Oh! Is there a local specialty?</I><P>
```

I don't actually speak French, German, Spanish, or Italian, but I guarantee the preceding set of questions will confuse just about any waiter in Europe. Figure 5-9 shows the result of the preceding formatting.

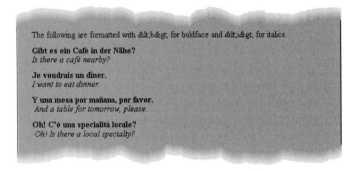

Figure 5-9: Language examples on the Web.

Some problems occur with the international characters supported in the basic HTML code, not the least of which is the fact that some significant elements are missing. If you want to write in Spanish, for example, you'll have to do without the upside-down question mark (¿)and the upside-down exclamation point (¡). If you want to denote currency, you can't code the yen (¥), the pound sterling (£), or even the cent sign (¢). Do you want to denote something that is registered or trademarked (® and ™)? You can't do that either within standard HTML.

The special characters in the preceding paragraph (and more) are added in the HTML+ extensions to HTML. I explain the many changes and updates in HTML+ compatible browsers in the last chapter of this book. If you want to peek now, flip to Chapter 12.

Comments within HTML Code

If you have spent any time working with complex markup languages such as HTML, you know that the ability to include tracking information and other comments can help you organize and remember your coding approach when you return to the pages later.

Fortunately, HTML supports a specific (if peculiar) notational format for comments within your documents. Any text surrounded by the elements <!– and –> is considered to be a comment and is ignored by Web browsers, as you can see in the following example:

```
<HTML>
<!– Last modified: 21 February 1995 –>
<TITLE>Enchilada Sauce</TITLE>
<!– inspired by an old recipe I heard in Mexico,
but I must admit that it's going to be very
different, because even the flour is subtly different
in Juarez and elsewhere than in the States . . . –>
<H1>Enchilada Sauce</H1>
```

When I feed the preceding text to a Web browser, the browser displays only one line of information, as you see in Figure 5-10.

tip You don't *have* to use comments, but if you're starting to build a complex Web space that offers many documents, just time-stamping each file could prove to be invaluable.

Figure 5-10: *Comments galore but none displayed.*

Table 5-2 contains a summary of all commands you learned in this chapter:

Table 5-2	HTML Tags Covered in This Chapter	
Tag	**Close Tag**	**Meaning**
<DD>	—	Definition description
<DIR>	</DIR>	Directory listing
<DL>	</DL>	Definition list
<DT>	—	Definition term
<LI>	—	List item
<MENU>	</MENU>	List of short items (can be formatted in multiple columns by the browser software)
<OL>	</OL>	Ordered (numbered) list
<UL>	</UL>	Unordered (bulleted) list
<!–	–>	Comments within HTML

Each chapter so far expands the depth and sophistication of your HTML skills. In this chapter, you learned about the various types of lists and how you can combine them — and many formatting tags — to produce very cool results. The next chapter is lots of fun. I show you the missing link — quite literally. Building on the explanation of URL formats in Chapter 2, the next chapter talks about how to add links to other Web sites and other places on the Internet.

Adding Pointers and Hot Links

This chapter talks about actual HTML pointers to other Web and Internet resources, shows you how to include pointers to graphics and illustrations, and builds on the URL explanation found in Chapter 2.

In this chapter

❑ Multiword HTML formatting tags
❑ Pointers to other Web pages
❑ Referencing non-Web information
❑ Pointers to your other pages

At this point, you should feel comfortable with your HTML composition skills. You certainly know all the key facets of HTML, with three notable exceptions; adding *links* to other documents, adding *internal links,* and adding *nontext* information to your pages. This chapter shows you how to add links; Chapters 7 and 8 cover links to internal references and graphics.

6

Much of this information builds on the extensive discussion of URLs (Uniform Resource Locators) in Chapter 2. You may want to skim that chapter again to refresh your memory before you proceed.

Multiword HTML Formatting Tags

So far, every document formatting tag that you've seen has looked like a couple of letters surrounded by angle brackets. But in fact, formatting tags can contain more information than just a few letters. All tags must begin with the open angle bracket, followed immediately by the *tag element;* no spaces are allowed. Inside the tag, however, you can specify other attributes in the format *attribute-name = value.*

One of the tags that you learned about earlier — <PRE>, for preformatted text — enables you to specify the set width that you'll be using, as shown in the following example:

```
It's a hot, hot day in the park, and lots of people
are wandering around without clothes on. Here's a
text picture of what I'm talking about:
<PRE WIDTH=5>
    +---------+
    | CENSORED |
    +---------+
</PRE>
<I>Sorry, but until all the releases are signed,
I can't let you see this picture.</I>
```

In the preceding HTML example, I deliberately added an error: I specified that the preformatted text should be shown with the assumption that the maximum width of each line of text is five characters (WIDTH=5). The actual output makes it clear that the browser ignores this particular facet of formatting, as Figure 6-1 shows.

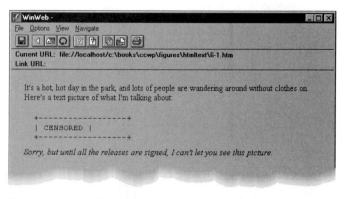

Figure 6-1: An HTML tag with attributes.

The preceding proves to be a great example of one of the challenges facing Web page designers. The formatting information that you specify in your HTML code may not be interpreted as you think it will be (as shown in figure 6-1) or at all (as in the request for multicolumn lists by the `<MENU>` formatting tag).

Fortunately, most of the other HTML tags work if you specify the appropriate attributes. You can specify anything you want within an HTML formatting tag; the browser interprets only those attributes that make sense within the context of that tag. (You can have fun with this, too. How about a format tag of `<P aragraph=right-justified>`? This tag works identically to the format tag `<P>` by itself, because the attribute `aragraph` is — no big surprise — meaningless.)

note

You can't have a space between the < and the tag name, but the elements are surrounded by spaces within.

Pointers to Other Web Pages

The basic HTML formatting tag for external references is `<A>`, the *anchor tag* (its ending partner is `</A>`). It *must* contain attributes. Without any attributes, the `<A>` tag has no meaning and doesn't affect the formatting of information. The following, for example, would result in the display of text without formatting:

```
You can now visit <A>the White House</A> on-line!
```

To make this link *live,* meaning to make it cause a browser to do something, you need to specify the *hypertext reference* attribute: HREF="value". The *value* can be empty if you don't know the actual information, but you must specify the attribute to make the link active. You can rewrite the sentence as follows to make it a Web link:

```
You can now visit <A HREF="">the White House</A> on-line!
```

The preceding line of HTML code would be displayed in a Web browser with the portion between the <A> references (the anchor tags) appearing in blue with an underline or highlighted in some other fashion. The information that should be contained between the quotation marks is the URL for the Web page you want to link to. The URL for the White House, for example, is http://www.whitehouse.gov/.

■ ■

One classic problem that appears in HTML code is the use of curly, smart, or fancy quotes; Web servers just don't know what they mean. Double check to ensure that the quotes in your HTML documents all have straight quotes: "like this" rather than "like this".

The following is the sentence with the correct, live hypertext link to the White House:

```
You can now visit <A HREF="http://www.whitehouse.gov/">the White House</
A> on-line!
```

The following is a more comprehensive example that combines various facets of HTML to build an interesting and attractive Web page:

```
<HTML>
<HEAD>
<TITLE>Visiting the White House and Other Government Sites</TITLE>
</HEAD>
<BODY>
In cyberspace, you can virtually travel anywhere. Of the various places
that are fun to check out, however, few are as interesting as the home
page for the <A HREF="http://www.whitehouse.gov/">White House</A>.
<H2>Government Sites on the Web</H2>

<UL>
<LI> <A HREF="http://naic.nasa.gov/fbi/FBI_homepage.html">Federal Bureau
of Investigation</A>
<LI> <A HREF="http://www.fedworld.gov/">FedWorld, a great starting point
for Government Research</A>
<LI> <A HREFf="http://novel.nifl.gov/">National Institute for Literacy
</A>
<LI> <A HREF="http://www.osmre.gov/">Office of Surface Mining Reclamation
and Enforcement</A>
<LI> <A HREF="http://www.sbaonline.sba.gov/">Small Business
Administration</A>
<LI> <A HREF="http://www.ssa.gov/">Social Security Administration</A>
<LI> <A HREF="http://web.fie.com/web/fed/aid/">U.S. Agency for
International Development (1)</A>
<LI> <A HREF="http://www.info.usaid.gov/">U.S. Agency for International
Development (2)</A>
</UL>
</BODY>
</HTML>
```

Figure 6-2 shows that the preceding HTML code is quite attractive when viewed in a browser (in this case, Netscape). The ugliness and confusion of the URLs are neatly hidden; readers can simply click on the name of an agency to connect directly to it.

Notice in Figure 6-2 that the link for the FBI page and the first link for the U.S. Agency for International Development are complex URLs with specified paths and pages. Also notice that the words *White House* in the prose at the beginning of the Web page now are highlighted and underlined, comprising a real Web link, too.

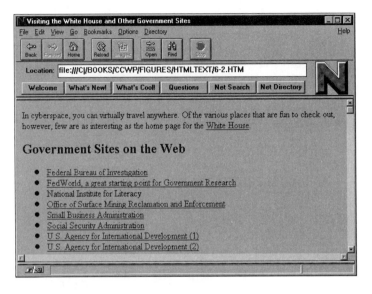

Figure 6-2: Government sites on the Web.

Understanding this section of this chapter is a terrific step forward in learning HTML. After you grasp how to build anchors, you'll be able to build Web "tables of contents," starting points for exploration on the Internet, with the best of them.

But how do you point to information that *isn't* another Web document? The next section shows you how.

Referencing Non-Web Information

To point to material that isn't a Web document, you simply use the appropriate URL, as specified in Chapter 2. If you learn, for example, that the FDIC (Federal Deposit Insurance Corporation) has a Gopher site but no Web site, and that the Gopher site is at `fdic.sura.net` on port 71, you could build a URL for it, as follows:

```
gopher://fdic.sura.net:71/
```

You then could drop the URL into your HTML code as a different value in an HREF attribute, as follows:

```
<A HREF="gopher://fdic.sura.net:71/">
```

The following example shows how the HTML code I discussed in the preceding section looks with the addition of the FDIC and the Consumer Product Safety Commission Gopher sites:

```
<HTML>
<HEAD>
<TITLE>Visiting the White House and Other Government Sites</TITLE>
</HEAD>
<BODY>
In cyberspace, you can virtually travel anywhere. Of the various places
that are fun to check out, few are as interesting as the home
page for the <A HREF="http://www.whitehouse.gov/">White House</A>.
<H2>Government Sites on the Web</H2>
<UL>
<LI> <A HREF="http://naic.nasa.gov/fbi/FBI_homepage.html">Federal Bureau
of Investigation</A>
<LI> <A HREF="gopher://fdic.sura.net:71/">Federal Deposit Insurance
Corporation</A>
<LI> <A HREF="http://www.fedworld.gov/">FedWorld, a great starting point
for government research</A>
<LI> <A HREF="http://novel.nifl.gov/">National Institute for Literacy</A>
<LI> <A HREF="http://www.osmre.gov/">Office of Surface Mining Reclamation
and Enforcement</A>
<LI> <A HREF="http://www.sbaonline.sba.gov/">Small Business
Administration</A>
<LI> <A HREF="http://www.ssa.gov/">Social Security Administration</A>
<LI> <A HREF="http://web.fie.com/web/fed/aid/">U.S. Agency for
International Development (1)</A>
<LI> <A HREF="http://www.info.usaid.gov/">U.S. Agency for International
Development (2)</A>
<LI> <A HREF="gopher://cpsc.gov/">U.S. Consumer Product Safety
Commission</A>
</UL>
</BODY>
</HTML>
```

In my Web browser (Netscape), the preceding looks almost identical to the earlier version, except that it has two new items listed (see Figure 6-3). This example underscores one of the real strengths of the HTML language: *all anchors* (hypertext pointers), regardless of the kind of information they point to, look the same on a Web page. No funny little Gopher icons appear next to the Gopher items, no FTP icons appear next to FTP archives, and so on. The pages contain uniform sets of pointers to other spots on the Internet that contain interesting, valuable, or fun resources.

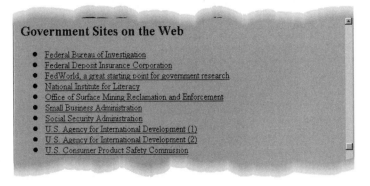

Figure 6-3: Which sites are Gopher sites?

Figure 1-7 in Chapter 1 showed how you can code various types of information in HTML format. I repeat that figure here as Figure 6-4.

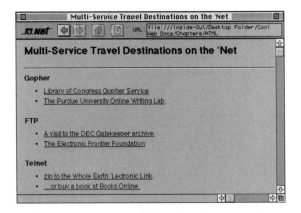

Figure 6-4: An example of non-Web links.

Now you can appreciate the figure's surprising hidden complexity, as shown in the following HTML code:

```
<HTML>
<HEAD>
<TITLE>Multi-service Travel Destinations on the 'Net</TITLE>
</HEAD><BODY>
<H1>Multi-service Travel Destinations on the 'Net</H1>
<I>Did I miss one? <A HREF="mailto:taylor@netcom.com">Drop me a note!
</A></I>
<HR>
<B>Gopher</B>
<UL>
<LI><A HREF="gopher://gopher.loc.gov/">Library of Congress Gopher
Service</A>
<LI><A HREF="gopher://owl.trc.purdue.edu/">The Purdue University Online
Writing Lab</A>
</UL>
<B>FTP</B>
<UL>
<LI><A HREF="ftp://gatekeeper.dec.com/">A visit to the DEC Gatekeeper
archive</A>
<LI><A HREF="ftp://ftp.eff.org/">The Electronic Frontier Foundation</A>
</UL>
<B>Telnet</B>
<UL>
<LI><A HREF="telnet://well.com/">zip to the Whole Earth 'Lectronic Link
</A>
<LI><A HREF="telnet://books.com/">... or buy a book at Books Online</A>
</UL>
<I>and various other services</I>
</BODY>
</HTML>
```

Of all the links demonstrated in this Web document, I think that the most notable is the `mailto:` link in the first line of text. Notice that the `mailto:` link is not presented as

```
<A HREF="mailto:taylor@netcom.com">Click here</A> to send me mail.
```

Instead, the link is smoothly and transparently integrated into the prose:

```
<A HREF="mailto:taylor@netcom.com">Drop me a note!</A></I>
```

Pointers to Your Other Pages

Being able to link to external information sources and sites on the Internet clearly is a huge boon to Web designers, but if you stopped at that and never learned any more, you'd be missing half the picture. The one piece that you still need to learn is how to reference other documents on your own server.

Although *personal* home pages often have a simple format similar to the examples in this chapter (that is, a few paragraphs about the person, perhaps a graphic or two, and then a list of favorite sites on the Web), more complex and sophisticated sites have a wide range of different Web documents available. These sites include the appropriate links to the other internal documents so that readers can easily jump among them.

There is an easy way and a hard way to reference internal documents (documents on your server). The hard way builds on the earlier examples: You figure out the full URL of each page and use those URLs as the hypertext reference tags. The easy way to reference another document on your server is to specify the document name only (or path and name) without any of the URL preface information. If you have a starting page called `home.html` and a second page called `resume.html`, for example, you could create the following link:

```
You're welcome to <A HREF="resume.html">read my resume</A>.
```

(Note: Purists would use the HTML code `r&eacute;sum&eacute;` instead of `resume`.)

Perhaps you want to make several files accessible on your Web server, and you want some sensible way to organize them. A hierarchical directory structure can prove to be a big advantage.

If you have a variety of information about the sandwiches and soups at the virtual deli featured in Chapter 5, you could organize that information as shown in Figure 6-5.

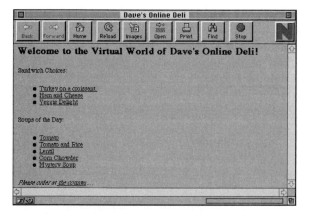

Figure 6-5: Organizing the deli menu data.

Now when people connect to the base URL (the address of the top-level menu itself), they see the formatted results of the following HTML code:

```
<HTML>
<HEAD>
<TITLE>Dave's On-Line Deli</TITLE>
</HEAD><BODY>
<H2>Welcome to the Virtual World of Dave's On-Line Deli!</H2>
Sandwich Choices:
<UL>
<LI><A HREF="sandwiches/turkey.html">Turkey on a croissant</A>
<LI><A HREF="sandwiches/ham.html">Ham and Cheese</A>
<LI><A HREF="sandwiches/veggie.html">Veggie Delight</A>
</UL>
Soups of the Day:
<UL>
<LI><A HREF="soups/tomato.html">Tomato</A>
<LI><A HREF="soups/tomato.html">Tomato and rice</A>
<LI><A HREF="soups/lentil.html">Lentil</A>
<LI><A HREF="soups/corn-chowder.html">Corn Chowder</A>
<LI><A HREF="soups/mystery.html">Mystery Soup</A>
</UL>
<I>Please order at <A HREF="order-counter.html">the counter</A> . . .
</I>
</BODY>
</HTML>
```

The new virtual-deli *home page* (which Web folks call the *root,* or the first page that visitors see when reaching a site) would be formatted as shown in Figure 6-5.

You can't see it in Figure 6-5, but the HTML code contains an error. To understand the problem — a relatively common one in complex lists — consider what happens if someone wants more information about the tomato soup instead of the tomato-and-rice soup. Both soup choices point to the same second page: `soups/tomato.html`.

If a Web user pops into the virtual deli and wants to find out more about the lentil soup, for example, he or she might click on the hypertext link `Lentil`. The user then would see another HTML document that provided information about the soup (and perhaps even included a picture of it). But how could you add a link back to the deli home page? Consider the following listing, paying close attention to the last few lines:

```
<HTML>
<HEAD>
<TITLE>Lentil Soup: A Cornerstone of the Virtual Deli</TITLE>
</HEAD>
<BODY>
<H1>Lentil Soup</H1>
It will come as no surprise to regular patrons of the Virtual Deli that
our lentil soup has quickly become one of the most popular items. With
its combination of six lentil beans, some succulent organic vegetables,
and our carefully filtered fresh spring water, a hot bowl of our lentil
soup on a cold day is unquestionably one of life's pleasures.
<P>
We'd love to tell you the recipe, too, but we feel that you really need
to come in and try it yourself.
<P>
<B>We recommend <A HREF="../sandwiches/veggie.html"> a veggie sandwich to
accompany it.</A></B>
<HR>
<A HREF="../deli.html">Back up to the main menu.</A>
</BODY>
</HTML>
```

When visitors to the virtual deli arrive at the page created by the preceding HTML text, they have moved down a level in the server's hierarchical directory structure, but they don't know that. The URLs in the document, however, tell the story. The main menu is `./deli.html`. The recommended sandwich to accompany the soup is in another directory — hence, its `./sandwiches` folder specification. See Figure 6-6 to see what the page looks like from a browser (winWeb).

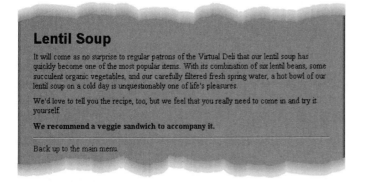

Lentil Soup

It will come as no surprise to regular patrons of the Virtual Deli that our lentil soup has quickly become one of the most popular items. With its combination of six lentil beans, some succulent organic vegetables, and our carefully filtered fresh spring water, a hot bowl of our lentil soup on a cold day is unquestionably one of life's pleasures.

We'd love to tell you the recipe, too, but we feel that you really need to come in and try it yourself.

We recommend a veggie sandwich to accompany it.

Back up to the main menu.

Figure 6-6: The lentil soup special.

In the previous listings, you can see the use of relative filename addresses. For example, "../deli.html" pops up one level in the file system to find the deli.html page. This makes for easy HTML coding but beware that problems can easily arise if you move any of the pages around without the rest of the files.

In this chapter, you learned how to include links to other sites on the World Wide Web and throughout the Internet. You also learned how to organize a set of Web documents in manageable folders and how to specify other documents on your own server with minimal fuss. The next chapter focuses on internal document references, which enable you to include a table of contents at the top of a large Web document. Chapter 7 also explains how to use internal document markers as hot links that enable people to jump to a specific spot in any Web document.

Internal Document References

This chapter shows you how to add a table of contents to a large Web document and use that table as a hot link to allow people to jump to a specific spot in that same or different document on your server.

In this chapter

- ☐ Defining Web-document jump targets
- ☐ Adding jump hot links to your Web pages
- ☐ Linking to jump targets in external documents

In Chapter 6, you learned about the anchor tag <A>; you also learned how to use the HREF attribute to build links to other pages on the World Wide Web. Another, equally valuable use for the <A> tag is the internal document reference, the focus of this chapter. You will find that as documents become larger, the capability to zoom (jump) to a predefined spot in a document can be invaluable.

Defining Web Document Jump Targets

I commented in Chapter 6 that the anchor tag `<A>` is the first of the HTML formatting tags that allow you to specify attributes. Note that rather than a format like `<URL="something"></URL>`, which would be more consistent with the other pieces of HTML, the format of the anchor tag is `<A something></A>`. This format is useful because some complex tags, particularly the instructions for including graphics, have dozens of variations. Imagine `<IMAGELEFTBOTTOM="imagefile">` or something similar. Instead, attributes were included in the design of HTML to allow a wide variety of different formats to be easily specified.

The greatest value of these attributes in formatting tags is that you can provide a wonderful sense of consistency in the interface and presentation of information. You can have half your links lead to other pages on the Web, with three links moving the reader farther down in the document and the rest of the links leading to other pages on your own server. The links will all have the same appearance (blue and underlined in most cases) and function (causing the browser to "jump" directly to the specified page.

Up to this point, the documents shown in this book have been short, with the majority of the information confined to the first screen of information within the browser. Such an approach to Web document design results in pages that are easy to navigate. Sometimes, however, it's impossible to keep a document from stretching over several pages.

If I wanted to write this chapter as an HTML document, I could make each section a different document. Even then, however, some of those sections would be sufficiently long that readers would be forced to scroll to find the information that they want.

A better layout is one in which the entire chapter is a single document, but the topic headers actually are links to the appropriate spots farther down in the page. Clicking on a table of contents entry like `Adding jump hot links to your Web page`, for example, would move you to that spot instantly. The challenge, of course, is to figure out when a certain length document is best as a single HTML file, and when it is best as a set of files. My rule of thumb is to move pages at logical jump points and to try and minimize load time for readers. This chapter could be a single HTML document, but the book itself would clearly be a set of documents.

The targets of internal Web document jumps are known as *anchors*. The HTML tag for an anchor point is another value for the `<A>` tag: `<A name=value>`. The *value* can be any sequence of characters, numbers, and punctuation marks, but I recommend that you stick with a strategy of mnemonic anchor names, such as *section1* or *references*. Some clients insist that all characters in the anchor be in lowercase, so you may want to experiment before you build a complex document.

The following example shows how a set of tags might look in a paper entitled "Sex Education: Morals versus Ethics." The anchors are built from the author names and years of publication, which then can be referenced as links in the rest of the document.

```
<A NAME="references">
<H3>References</H3>
<OL>
<LI><A NAME="driskill-delampo92">
Driskill, P., &amp; Delampo, R. L. (1992). Sex education in the 1990's: A
systems perspective on family sexuality. <I>Journal of Sex Education and
Therapy</i>, 18, 175-185.
<LI><A name="dewitt93">
Elmer-DeWitt, P. (1993). Making the case for abstinence. <I>Time
</I>, 141(5), 64-65.
<LI><A name="fay-gordon92">
Fay, G., &amp; Gordon, S. (1992). Moral sexuality education and
democratic values. <I>Theory into Practice</I>, 28, 211-216.
<LI><A name="gibbs93">
Gibbs, N. (1993). How should we teach our children about sex? <I>
Time</I>, 141(5), 60-66.
<LI><A name="gordon90">
Gordon, S. (1990). Sexuality education in the 1990s. <I>Health
Education</I>, 21, 4-5.
<LI><A name="gordon91">
Gordon, S. (1991). Sex education-What we're doing wrong. <I>The
Humanist</I>, Sep/Oct, 43-44.
<LI><A name="greenberg90">
Greenberg, J. S. (1990). Preparing teachers for sexuality education.
<I>Theory into Practice</I>. 28, 227-232.
<LI><A name="gudorf91">
Gudorf, C. (1991). Are you giving your kids double messages about sex?
<I>U. S. Catholic</I>, 56(9), 20-27.
<LI><A name="haffner90">
Haffner, D. W. (1990). AIDS and sexuality education. <I>Theory into
Practice</I>, 28, 198-202.
<LI><A name="hale92">
Hale, J. P. (1992). Sex ed, up to date. <I>National Review</I>, May 25,
31-33.
<LI><A name="kirby93">
Kirby, D. (1993). Research on effectiveness of sex education programs.
<I>Theory into Practice</I>, 28, 165-171.
</OL>
```

Viewed in a Web browser (see Figure 7-1), the preceding document looks like an attractive list of journal references. Because anchors are destinations on the current page rather than links to go elsewhere, the text between the <A NAME> and </A> is not highlighted in any way when displayed.

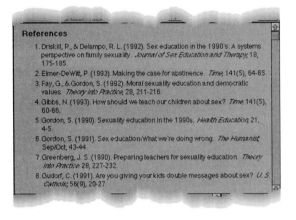

Figure 7-1: References from a sex-education paper.

What I've done in the example here is not only add links to each of the reference citations but also add a link to the references section itself, which could then be easily included as part of a table of contents to the document. This would offer readers the chance to jump directly to the opening arguments, supporting arguments, conclusions, or, in this case, the references section of the document.

Adding Jump Links to Your Web Pages

The partner of an anchor in HTML documents is the formatting tag that defines the *jump*, or active link within the document. It's a variant on the <A> format that you're already familiar with; the tag turns out to be another HREF hypertext reference, this time with the URL replaced by the anchor name prefaced by a pound sign (#).

For example, if the *anchor* that you want to connect is specified as <A NAME="references">, you would specify the *jump* as <A HREF="#references">go to reference info</A>.

In creating cool Web documents, the goal is to avoid phrases like the following:

```
<A HREF="#references">Click here</A> to see the references.
```

Instead, try to integrate the references more smoothly into the text, as follows:

```
<A HREF="#references">References and Bibliography</A>.
```

For a document that discusses ingredients for mixed fruit drinks, for example, the HTML source might look like the following:

```
<H2>Ingredients for an Energy Blend</H2>
<UL>
<LI><A HREF="#strawberry">Strawberries</A>
<LI><A HREF="#blueberry">Blueberries</A>
<LI><A HREF="#mango">Mango</A>
<LI><A HREF="#banana">Bananas</A>
<LI><A HREF="#raspberry">Raspberries</A>
<LI><A HREF="#peach">Peaches</A>
</UL>
```

This list would be formatted attractively, as Figure 7-2 shows. The format is identical to the way the information would be presented if the links were external, perhaps even on different servers on the Web.

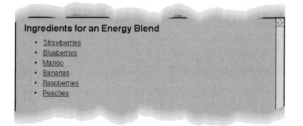

Figure 7-2: Energy-blend ingredients.

For a different way to use internal references, examine the following snippet from the main section of the sex-education paper, which includes internal links to the anchors in the references section. Notice that an anchor also has been assigned to the section head.

```
Seven values for holistic sexuality education have been proposed, ranging
from the observation that sexual decisions should support the dignity,
equality, and worth of each individual and that parenthood requires many
responsibilities that adolescents are usually unable to assume, to the
idea that it's usually preferable for adolescents to refrain from sexual
intercourse (<A HREF="#fay-gordon92">Fay &amp; Gordon, 1992</A>).
<P>
<A NAME="the-debate">
<H2>The Debate over Research Findings</H2>
Research on sex education curricula is controversial. Values and Choices
has been studied in various settings, and while initial post-course
attitudes of students demonstrated they were significantly more support-
ive of abstinence and significantly less likely to <I>intend to</I>
engage in sexual intercourse, followup interviews four months later
revealed that the differences between the group and national norms was no
longer statistically significant (<A HREF="#kirby90">Kirby, 1990</A>).
Many educators also observe that none of the pro-abstinence-only cur-
ricula research has been submitted to peer-review journals (<A
HREFf="#tapia93">Tapia, 1993</A>).
<P>
One research project, oft-quoted by abstinence-only supporters demon-
strated that pregnancy rates among students having taken the Sex Respect
program at a San Diego school were an impressive 45-percent lower than
those that hadn't. Later research by the San Diego <I>Union</I>, however,
found that much of the information had been fabricated
(<A HREF="#dewitt93">Elmer-DeWitt, 1993</A>, <A HREF="#tapia93">Tapia,
1993</A>).
<P>
```

In a browser, the paper is displayed in a format that is quite pleasing to the eye and easy to navigate. All the hot links and anchor information are appropriately hidden from view or sufficiently subtle that the reader can focus on the material itself (see Figure 7-3).

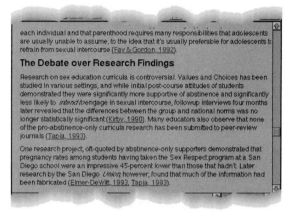

Figure 7-3: The research paper with reference hot links.

When scholars first envisioned the need for citations in research, to defend and explain where particular views and ideas originate, what they dreamed of is surprisingly close to what we now can include in Web documents. If you are surprised by something in such a paper, or if the paper whetted your appetite for a more extensive treatment of the subject, you can click on the author citation. You then instantly move to the references section, and the appropriate citation is shifted to the top of the screen so that you can identify the information that you seek.

Figure 7-4 shows what would happen if you wanted more information on the Elmer-DeWitt article and clicked the `<A HREF="#dewitt93">` link.

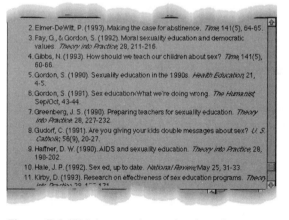

Figure 7-4: Web browser jumped to the references.

One thing to keep in mind when you specify your anchor points is the fact that the *exact* spot of the reference becomes the top of the displayed document. A sequence like the following shows the possible danger therein:

```
<H2>Bananas</H2>
<A NAME="BANANAS">
The banana is one of the most exotic, yet most easily purchased, fruits
in the world.
```

The raw Web document is attractively formatted, but the resulting behavior will not be what you seek: users who jump to the "#BANANA" tag will have the preceding sentence in the first line of their displays; the <H2> header will be one line off-screen. A much better idea is to flip the two items, as follows:

```
<A NAME="BANANAS">
<H2>Bananas</H2>
The banana is one of the most exotic, yet most easily purchased, fruits
in the world.
```

Always test your Web documents before unleashing them on the world. I can't overemphasize this. Subtle problems with where your anchor tags are placed, for example, are classic mistakes found in otherwise cool Web pages.

Jumping Into Organized Lists

Anchors and jump points also are commonly used to help readers navigate large lists of alphabetically sorted information. Consider the following simple phone book layout:

```
<TITLE>Jazz Institute Internal Phone Book</TITLE>
<H1>Jazz Institute Internal Phone Book</H1>
<P>
Section Shortcut:
<A HREF="#a-c">[A-C]</A>
<A HREF="#d-h">[D-H]</A>
<A HREF="#i-l">[I-L]</A>
<A HREF="#m-n">[M-N]</A>
<A HREF="#o-s">[O-S]</A>
<A HREF="#t-z">[T-Z]</A><BR>
<H2><A name="a-c">A-C</H2>
Benson, George  (x5531)<BR>
Coleman, Ornette  (x5143)<BR>
Coltrane, John  (x5544)
<H2><a name="d-h">D-H</H2>
Dorsey, Tom  (x9412)<BR>
Ellington, Duke (x3133)<BR>
Getz, Stan  (x1222)<BR>
<H2><A name="i-l">I-L</H2>
Jackson, Milt  (x0434)<BR>
Laffite, Guy (x5358) <BR>
<H2><a name="m-n">M-N</H2>
Monk, Thelonious  (x3333)<BR>
Noone, Jimmie (x5123)<BR>
<H2><A name="o-s">O-S</H2>
Parker, Charlie  (x4141)<BR>
Peterson, Oscar  (x8983)<BR>
Reinhardt, Django  (x5351)<BR>
<H2><a name="t-z">T-Z</H2>
Taylor, Billy  (x3311)<BR>
Tyner, McCoy  (x4131)<BR>
Waller, Fats  (x1321)<BR>
```

Although the HTML in the preceding example appears to be complex, Figure 7-5 shows that the result not only looks cool but is also useful.

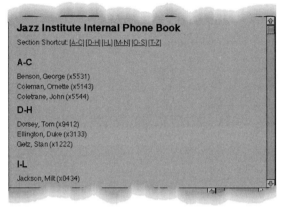

Figure 7-5: The Jazz Institute phone book.

You can start to get a feeling for how complex HTML text can become if you imagine that each entry in the phone list actually is a link to that person's home page or other material somewhere else on the Web. Every line of information displayed could be the result of four or more lines of HTML.

Linking to Jump Targets in External Documents

Now that you're familiar with the concept of jumping around within a single document, you'll be glad to hear that you can also add the *#anchor* notation to the end of any Web URL to make that link move directly to the specific anchor point in the document.

Suppose, for example, that the sex-education paper resided on a system called `research.educ.purdue.edu` and that its full URL was `http://research.educ.purdue.edu/Students/Taylor,D/500D/sex-ed.html`.

A visit to the page reveals that a variety of anchor tags are embedded therein, including the references tag at the beginning of the references section of the paper. You could link directly to that spot from another Web page, as in the following example:

```
Other people on the Internet have chosen different references
for their exploration of the ethical issues surrounding
sex education in the United States. One example is the article
<A HREF="http://research.educ.purdue.edu/Students/Taylor,D/500D/
sex-ed.html">Sex Education: Morals or Ethics?</A> by
Dave Taylor, with his extensive
<A HREF="http://research.educ.purdue.edu/Students/Taylor,D/500D/
sex-ed.html#references">set of references</A>.
Other sources to explore include . . .
```

The prose is displayed in a Web browser as you would expect. Figure 7-6 shows that the HREF that includes the specific internal link #references is displayed as just a link, underlined and in blue.

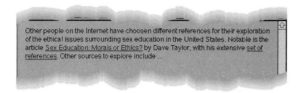

Figure 7-6: One of these two link to the external anchor.

Pointing to external anchors can be useful for linking to large Web documents which contain a great deal of information that may confuse your reader. Be careful, though; if anyone but you maintains the anchors, the names may change, the documents may be reorganized, or other changes may suddenly invalidate your links *without your even knowing about it.* There's always a chance that a whole document will vanish from the Web, of course, but the chance that a link *within* a document will change is considerably higher.

This chapter introduced two useful devices for organizing and navigating large Web documents: internal anchors and links to those anchors. The same links can be accessed as part of a general Web URL, but beware: Anchor names may change or move without your knowledge, thereby invalidating your connection. The next chapter shows you how to make your Web pages even more visually appealing by adding graphics. The chapter includes some hints on software that you can use to create the graphics, whether you're on a PC, Macintosh, or UNIX workstation.

Jazzing Up Web Pages

This chapter shows you how to jazz up your Web pages
with multimedia elements and includes discussion of how to
create and edit graphic images, audio, and even video clips.

In this chapter

- ❏ Including images in Web documents
- ❏ Text alternatives for nongraphical users
- ❏ Image-alignment options
- ❏ Stealing images off the Net
- ❏ Scanned photographs
- ❏ Transparent colors
- ❏ Audio, video and other media

This is the only chapter in the book that contains platform-specific
information. Here you will learn about graphical editors and GIF translators for Macintosh, PC/Windows, and UNIX systems.

You have learned enough HTML by this point to make you dangerous: You should be able to create complex webs of information with sophisticated text formatting.

But that isn't all there is to Web design; the missing ingredient in this soup is *graphics*. The capability to place large and small images — and even to make the images hypertext references — is a crucial element of cool Web-page design. Not to mention that it's great fun to have Web pages with pictures, audio, and even video snippets!

In this chapter, I diverge slightly from the platform-independent approach that I have taken in this book so far and delve into some specifics of creating graphics and images for Windows, Macintoshes, and UNIX workstations. Most of the examples in this chapter were created with programs that are available for both Macintosh and Windows machines.

Including Images in Web Pages

Including images in a Web document is remarkably easy with the <IMG> (image) format tag. One limitation, though, is that you can use only two *graphics formats* within a document. (By "within a document" I mean that the image can be viewed within a Web browser — *inline*, as it's called in the desktop publishing and layout world). The two formats supported by HTML are

❑ GIF: CompuServe's Graphics Interchange Format

❑ JPEG: The industry-standard Joint Photographic Expert Group format

If you have graphics in another format — for example, TIFF, PCX, or PICT — a user at the other end of the Web wire *may* be able to display those graphics, but only in a separate application, which may or may not automatically be launched by the user's Web browser.

> **["" "]**
>
> I pronounce GIF and JPEG as "jiff" and "jay-peg." Your friends, though, may well look at you oddly if you start talking about "gorgeous jiffs and small jay-pegs" on your Web pages.

Some Web browsers support only the GIF format, which has become the de facto standard for graphics in cool Web pages. GIF is a great thing, and the addition of support for graphics clearly has been a boon to the Web, but many of the most powerful graphics programs don't support the GIF format. Why? Typical graphics programs support PICT (for the Mac), TIFF, BMP, and PCX (for Windows), and various proprietary formats, but supporting GIF requires software developers to license the encoding technologies separately, which most of those companies are loath to do.

So, for your Web pages, you want your images to be in GIF format. Fortunately, a variety of freeware and shareware programs — all available on the net — can translate common graphics formats into GIF format. For the Mac, I recommend GIFConverter or GraphicConverter; for Windows systems, you can use PaintShop Pro or Lview.

Some great starting points for finding graphics software packages are

❑ Yahoo: http://www.yahoo.com/Computers/Software/Graphics

❑ Yahoo: http://www.yahoo.com/Computers/World_Wide_Web/Programming

❑ Yahoo: http://www.yahoo.com/Computers/Internet/Archie

❑ Archie database: http://www.thegroup.net/AA.html

When you have a GIF file, the <IMG> tag is used to place that file in the text. Suppose that I have a file called black-box.gif that I want to use as the opening graphic in my Web page. The following example shows how this file might appear in an HTML document:

```
<HTML>
<HEAD>
<TITLE>The Dark Box</TITLE>
</HEAD><BODY>
<IMG SRC="black-box.gff">
<H1>Welcome to the Dark Box</H1>
There are boxes that aren't very well lit,
there are boxes that might even be
sealed, but I guarantee that you've never seen
anything quite as terrifying as
<I>The Dark Box</I>.
<P>
Dare you continue? <A HREF="blackbox2.html">yes</A> no.
</BODY>
</HTML>
```

As you can see, <IMG> is a formatting tag that allows you to specify different values. This tag proves to be vital as you learn more about its capabilities. The one variable that must appear in the <IMG> tag is a specification of the GIF source file itself, in the format SRC=filename.

Figure 8-1 shows how the preceding HTML snippet appears when viewed in a browser.

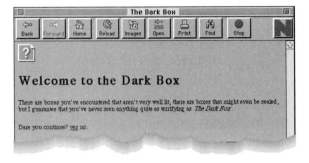

Figure 8-1: Graphics specified but not loaded.

The small box in Figure 8-1 that contains the ? is in fact *not* the graphic that I wanted to include but an indication from the browser that an inline graphic was specified with the `<IMG>` tag but was not *loaded*. In this case, the graphic was not loaded because I mistyped the name of the graphics file, specifying `blackbox.gff` rather than `blackbox.gif`. A mistake like that is another good reason to test your Web pages extensively before letting other users visit it.

To correct the problem, I fixed the spelling. Figure 8-2 shows what the resulting Web page looks like with all the information properly loaded (more attractive than with the unloaded graphic, eh?).

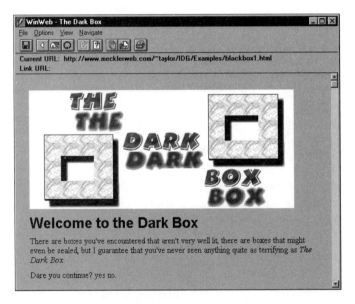

Figure 8-2: The Dark Box Web page.

You may have a fast connection to the Internet, but remember that many people are trapped with very slow dial-up connections at 9600 baud or — horrors! — slower. Prodigy, America Online, and CompuServe users can access Web pages, but performance can be quite slow. Also bear in mind that, to speed up access, many users simply skip loading the graphics unless they have to do so to understand a page.

A popular use of graphics involves using icons instead of text tags. If I had two GIF files — yes.gif and no.gif — here's how I could spiff up the Dark Box page:

```
<HTML>
<HEAD>
<TITLE>The Dark Box</TITLE>
</HEAD><BODY>
<IMG SRC="black-box.gif">
<H1>Welcome to the Dark Box</H1>
There are boxes that aren't very well lit,
there are boxes that might even be
sealed, but I guarantee that you've never seen
anything quite as terrifying as
<I>The Dark Box</I>.
<P>
Dare you continue? <A HREF="blackbox2.html">
<IMG SRC="yes.gif"></A> <IMG SRC="no.gif">
</BODY>
</HTML>
```

The icons and graphics that are included in this image (that is, yes.gif and no.gif) are separate files in the same directory as the Web page. Figure 8-3 shows the new, cooler Web page with all graphics included.

A page in which graphics are a vital part of the design, however, can end up looking peculiar to a large percentage of Web users since many people either cannot, or opt not to, download them when viewing Web pages. That fact makes for a design dilemma: should pages be designed to omit the graphics, include them as critical, or just as addenda?

Some Internet pundits tell you to just go wild with the graphics, because within a few months, everyone will have a fast, powerful computer and a high-speed connection. I don't agree with that advice. Because the GIF format, which is already compressed, still produces large graphics files, you should ensure that people who omit the images still see a meaningful page.

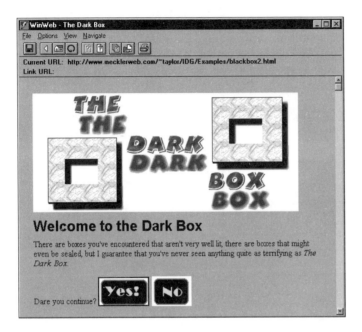

Figure 8-3: The cooler Dark Box page.

 A good design strategy is to preview your page without any graphics loaded, to see how everything looks and to ensure that the page makes sense.

Text Alternatives for Text-Based Web Browsers

Although the most popular browsers — Netscape and Mosaic — offer lots of graphics, there is also an important Web browser called Lynx that is designed for text-only display; Lynx is found most commonly on UNIX systems where users have dial-up accounts. Even at a very slow connect speed, Lynx allows many users to navigate the Web and have fun.

With Lynx, graphics can't be included in the display. So an additional option is allowed in the HTML <IMG> format tag. ALT=text is the magic sequence. Whatever text replaces *text* is displayed if the user can't view graphics.

To understand why the ALT = element is necessary, see Figure 8-4, which shows how the Dark Box page would appear in Lynx.

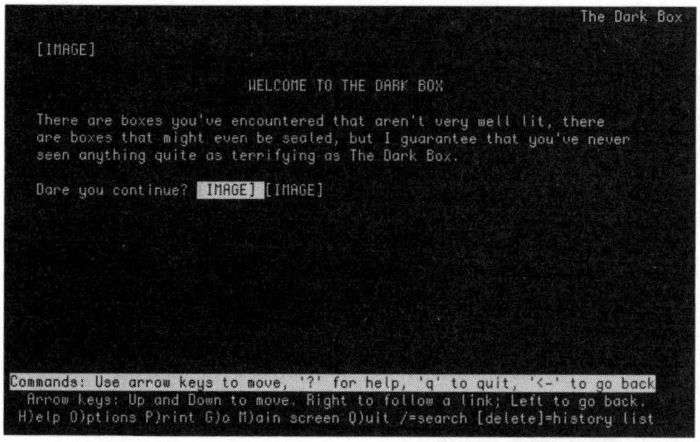

Figure 8-4: The Dark Box in Lynx's text-only display.

The user faces a problem, obviously: which of the images at the bottom, both of which are hypertext references, represents the answer Yes? As it is, there's no way to tell. That problem is why you should always include some meaningful information in the ALT variable. The following example shows how a slight rewrite of the HTML code makes the page clear to a text-only user:

```
<HTML>
<HEAD>
<TITLE>The Dark Box</TITLE>
</HEAD><BODY>
<IMG SRC="black-box.gif" ALT="[wicked cool graphic]">
<H1>Welcome to the Dark Box</H1>
There are boxes that aren't very well lit,
there are boxes that might even be
sealed, but I guarantee that you've never seen
anything quite as terrifying as
<I>The Dark Box</I>.
<P>
Dare you continue? <A HREF="blackbox2.html">
<IMG SRC="yes.gif" ALT="<yes>"></A> <IMG SRC="no.gif" ALT="<no>">
</BODY>
</HTML>
```

When displayed within Lynx, the preceding offers meaningful and helpful information that allows users to work with the page and explore the Dark Box, even when they're missing the graphic image (see Figure 8-5).

Figure 8-5: The Dark Box, text-only version.

Unfortunately, if a user opts not to auto-load images in a graphic browser such as Netscape or winWeb (perhaps because the connection is slow), he or she usually doesn't get the helpful text information — only the generic graphic shown in Figure 8-1.

> **tip**
> You don't *have* to place brackets, parentheses, or anything else around the text in the ALT= section of the <IMG SRC> tag, but in my experience brackets or parentheses help users figure out the page (and look better as well).

Image Alignment Options

Go back to the first section of this chapter and refer to Figure 8-3. Look carefully at the relative alignment of the text Dare you continue? with the Yes! and No icons. The text is aligned with the bottoms of the icons, which looks good.

But what if you want a different alignment? Or what if you use different alignments for multiple graphics? You can specify a third variable in the <IMG> formatting tag, ALIGN, which gives you precise control over alignment.

You can use the alignment options `ALIGN=top`, `ALIGN=middle`, and `ALIGN=bottom`. By default, images and adjacent text are aligned at the bottom, as you can see in Figure 8-3. The following HTML snippet demonstrates all three alignment options:

```
<H1>IMG Alignment Options</H1>
<H2>ALIGN=top</H2>
Dare you continue? <A HREF="blackbox2.html">
<IMG SRC="yes.GIF" ALIGN=top></A>
(be careful! This takes courage!)
<H2>ALIGN=middle</H2>
Dare you continue? <A HREF="blackbox2.html">
<IMG SRC="yes.GIF" ALIGN=middle></A>
(be careful! This takes courage!)
<H2>ALIGN=bottom</H2>
Dare you continue? <A HREF="blackbox2.html">
<IMG SRC="yes.GIF" ALIGN=bottom></A>
(be careful! This takes courage!)
```

Figure 8-6 shows this example in a Web browser.

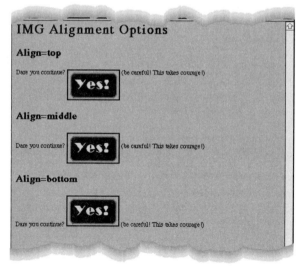

Figure 8-6: Image-alignment options.

The preceding example demonstrates the options for a graphic surrounded by text. However, you may want to align the Yes! and No buttons at the bottom and to align the preceding text with the *centers* of the two icons. The following example shows two ways to accomplish this task:

```
Dare you continue? <A HREF="blackbox2.html">
<IMG SRC="yes.GIF" ALIGN=middle></A>
<IMG SRC="no.GIF" ALIGN=bottom>
(be careful! This takes courage!)
```

Upon looking at this seemingly reasonable HTML snippet in a Web browser, I realize that the code doesn't do what I want it to do. Figure 8-7 shows the rather cheery and festive, albeit incorrect, result.

Dare you continue? **Yes!** **No** (be careful! This takes courage!)

Figure 8-7: So much for aligning the icons.

The truth is that centering text on bottom-aligned graphics is beyond the capability of HTML 1.0 (current version at time of this writing), as well as the latest specification document. At best, you could make all your icons a single graphic element and then use an ISMAP tag to tell your server which area corresponds to which option. (See Chapter 12 for information on ISMAP graphics.)

When you lay out your graphics, remember that different browsers have different screen widths and that they move elements around to fit that screen width. A classic mistake in an otherwise cool Web page is previewing it with a relatively narrow window and thinking that it looks great. However, a user with a huge screen width would see all the graphics and text bubble up toward the top — an arrangement that ruins the overall appearance of the page.

tip ■

A simple rule of thumb for images: If you don't want any material to appear after the graphic, add a <BR> tag to the end of the HTML sequence that specifies the graphic.

A Few Real World Examples

This section examines some interesting graphics and layout options that people are using on the Web for their own cool designs.

The first example is the home page of Computer Literacy Bookshops of California (`http://www.clbooks.com/`). This low-key home page contains a small number of icons and offers a good demonstration of the `ALIGN=top` option. Figure 8-8 shows the top of the home page.

Figure 8-8: Computer Literacy on the Web.

The following HTML code is used to generate Computer Literacy's home page, something easily seen by choosing the Options ⇨ View Source capability in winWeb or MacWeb, or, if you're using Netscape, try View ⇨ Source...:

```
<HTML>
<HEAD>
<TITLE>Computer Literacy Bookshops Home Page</TITLE>
</HEAD><BODY>
<IMG SRC="3dmast.gif" ALT=""><P>
<H1>Computer Literacy Bookshops Home Page</H1>
Welcome! Our Web Server was designed with functionality, not glitz, as
the highest priority. Please, let us know how we are doing and what we
can do to improve our service!
<A HREF="mailto:webmaster@clbooks.com"><I>webmaster@clbooks.com</I></A>
<HR>
<DL>
<DT><H2><A HREF="/news/newatclb.html">
<IMG SRC="/icons/book-small.gif" ALIGN="top" ALT="[*]"> What's New at
Computer Literacy?</A></H2>
<DD>Information on special free events, trade shows, new services, and
other topical information. <B>Updated Wednesday, 15 March 1995</B>
<DT><H2><A HREF="/clbinfo/aboutclb.html">
 <IMG SRC="/icons/book-small.gif" ALIGN="top" ALT="[*]"> Store Informa-
tion and Services</A></H2>
<DD>Phone numbers, fax, email address, directions to our store locations,
and a list of services Computer Literacy provides.
<DT><H2><A HREF="/nbb/nbbindex.html">
 <IMG SRC="/icons/book-small.gif" ALIGN="top" ALT="[*]"> New Book Bulle-
tins, Updates, and Galley Alley</A></H2>
<DD>Our latest New Book Bulletins in hypermedia format and various re-
lated files, including an interview with Donald Knuth, and a list of some
hot forthcoming titles in Galley Alley (sm)!
```

note

Don't forget that the <DL> format is a *definition list* and that entries have a <DT> defined term and a <DD> definition.

The next interesting site, *PC Week*, has even fewer graphics and replaces the boring black bullet with a neat red sphere. Figure 8-9 shows the top of the *PC Week* Web page, located at http://www.ziff.com/~pcweek.

The HTML used to create the page in Figure 8-9 includes a variety of tags that are specific to the Netscape browser, but the figure shows this page from within MacWeb, which simply ignores all formatting tags that it doesn't understand. Following is the code used:

```
<HTML>
<HEAD>
<TITLE>PC Week</TITLE>
</HEAD>
<BODY>
<IMG ALT="PC Week" SRC="http://www.ziff.com/~eamonn/icons/logotr1.gif">
<BR>
<H4><B><I>The National Newspaper of Corporate Computing — World-Wide Web
edition</I></B></H4><P>
<HR>
<P>
<CENTER><I>Updated March 17, 1995 7:52 AM E.T.</I></CENTER><P>
<DL>
<H4><DT><IMG ALT="o" src="/~eamonn/icons/redball.gif"><A HREF="http://
www.ziff.com/~pcweek/daily/coop/cc0317.html"> Coop's Corner</A></H4>
<DD><I>March 17: </I>Mystery deepens in case involving Gates' mother
<H4><DT><IMG ALT="o" src="/~eamonn/icons/redball.gif"><A HREF="http://
www.ziff.com/~pcweek/news/mar_1995/news_thay_0316.html"> NCD to deliver
all-in-one Internet front-end ware</A></H4>
<DD>Mariner software is for users who don't want to learn six or seven
different protocols, applications
<H4><DT><IMG ALT="o" src="/~eamonn/icons/redball.gif"><A HREF="http://
www.ziff.com/~pcweek/news/mar_1995/news_tyam_0316.html"> NeXT's Martin
Yam on linking objects, platforms</A></H4>
<DD>Predicts continued growth in Unix server market
```

 ■
Notice the tags `<CENTER>` and `</CENTER>`, which are used to center text on the screen in a certain Web browser. The `<CENTER>` tags are discussed in detail in Chapter 9, which focuses on the Netscape extensions and how they can help you produce very cool Web pages.

An interesting decision that the designers of the *PC Week* Web site made was to show all hypertext references as *full* reference URLs rather than in the more succinct *relative* reference form. For example, the link for "Coop's Corner" reads `http://www.ziff.com/~pcweek/daily/coop/cc0317.html`, but because the base address of this page is `http://www.ziff.com/~pcweek`, the link could just as easily have been written in the format `<a href="daily/coop/cc0317.html">`, which would have been easier to work with. Frankly, the best approach is to have all local URLs specified relative to the root server, so in this case they'd use `/~pcweek/daily/coop/cc0317.html`. An even better reason to use the short version would be that, if the entire site were renamed for any reason, there would be no need to modify each and every link in every document on the site.

Figure 8-9: *PC Week* on the Web.

A third site worth checking out, the Wentworth Gallery, has some great graphics with interesting alignments, an attractive interface, and uses simple HTML code to boot. Wentworth Gallery features a variety of lithographs and other artwork, as you can see in Figure 8-10.

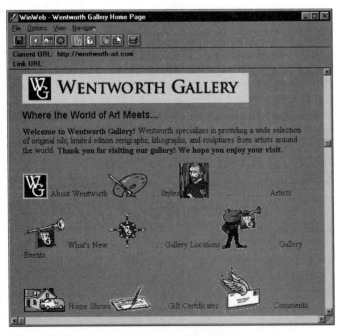

Figure 8-10: Wentworth Gallery on the Web.

Following is the remarkably clean HTML that generates the page seen in Figure 8-10:

```
<HTML>
<TITLE>Wentworth Gallery Home Page</TITLE>
<H2><IMG SRC=/wwg/admin/gifs/home_p.gif>
<P>Where the World of Art Meets...</H2>
<P>
<B>Welcome to Wentworth Gallery! </B>As the largest fine art gallery
chain in the United States,
<A HREF=/wwg/admin/aboutwwg.htm>Wentworth Gallery </A>
is delighted to add this cyberspace gallery to the 37
other galleries we operate throughout the United States.
Wentworth specializes in providing a wide selection of
original oils, limited edition serigraphs, lithographs,
and sculptures from artists around the world.
<B>Thank you for visiting our gallery!
We hope you enjoy your visit.</B><P>
<IMG SRC="/wwg/admin/gifs/news.gif"><A HREF="/wwg/admin/news.htm">What's
New</A> . . . .
<IMG SRC="/wwg/admin/gifs/styles.gif">
<A HREF="/wwg/gallery/styles.htm">Styles</A>
     . . . . . . . . . . . . .
<IMG SRC="/wwg/admin/gifs/artists.gif">
<A HREF="/wwg/gallery/artists.htm">Artists</A>
<P>
<IMG SRC="/wwg/admin/gifs/shows.gif"><A HREF="/wwg/admin/
home_sh.htm">Home Shows</A> . . . .
<IMG SRC="/wwg/admin/gifs/locate.gif">
<A HREF="/wwg/admin/locate.htm">Gallery Locations</A> . . .
<IMG SRC="/wwg/admin/gifs/gifts.gif">
<A HREF="/wwg/admin/gifts.htm">Gift Certificates</A>
<P>
<IMG SRC="/wwg/admin/gifs/740x2.gif">
<P>
<I>(c) Copyright 1995, Wentworth Gallery</I><BR>
<I>gallery@wentworth-art.com</I>
```

The biggest problem with the preceding HTML code is that it doesn't end correctly: there's no </HTML> tag. The lack of <HEAD> and <BODY> section isn't as great a problem; most Web browsers seem to be quite forgiving of omissions, but over time more and more will insist on the <HTML></HTML> pair to verify that the information received is, in fact, an HTML document.

Did you catch the error in the page design? Each of the small icons along the bottom has an associated text tag — a great idea. But there's no way to lock the icon with the text, so the actual text for the last icon ends up in the wrong place. (Refer to Figure 8-10 to see where Gift Certificates ended up because of the width of my window.)

I'll end this section with a more complex image-alignment example of my own, for an online tutorial that I've been working on in my (copious) spare time. The goal of this page is to display a variety of common icons and explain what they do. Here's the source HTML for the Web page:

```
<HTML>
<HEAD>
<TITLE>An Introduction to Mac Icons</TITLE>
</HEAD><BODY>
<H1>Intro to Macintosh Icons</H1>
<I>Some of these are System 7.x only...</I>
<P>
<DL>
<DT><IMG SRC="generic-file.gif"><B>GENERIC FILE ICON</B>
<DD>This is a generic file — that is, one that doesn't have any a
pplication ownership information stored in the Mac file system or its own
resource fork. Opening these files typically results in the use of the
<B>TeachText</B> or <B>SimpleText</B> application, if possible, although
you can fine tune that with the new <B>Easy Launch</B> control panel.
<DT><IMG SRC="generic-folder.gif"><B>GENERIC FOLDER ICON</B>
<DD>This is a standard folder icon on the Macintosh. Folders can contain
just about anything, including files, applications, and other folders.
Opening a folder results in the display of the contents of that folder in
a separate window on the Macintosh.
<DT><IMG SRC="system-folder.gif"><B>SYSTEM FOLDER ICON</B>
<DD>A special folder at the top level of each hard disk on the Macintosh
is the <I>System Folder</I>. This folder contains all the files,
applications, and information needed to run and maintain the Macintosh
operating system and all the goodies therein. The tiny Mac icon inside
the folder indicates that this particular <I>System Folder</I> is
<I>live</I> and that the information inside was used to start the current
Macintosh.
<P>
You can find many files in the <B>System Folder</B>, including the
following:
<DL>
<DT><IMG SRC="apple-menu.gif"><B>APPLE MENU FOLDER ICON</B>
<DD>
Ever wondered where all the information that shows up on the Apple menu
(the menu that you see when you click the <IMG SRC="apple-icon.gif"> at
the left end of the menu bar)? They're all just files, folders,
applications, and aliases tucked into the Apple folder itself. Open this
folder sometime, and compare the contents with the result of clicking the
Apple icon itself.
```

Figure 8-11 shows the result. Notice that the use of the definition list gave me a nice indentation style, without any hassle.

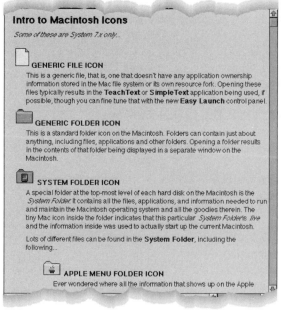

Figure 8-11: The icon tour.

Where Do You Get Images From?

Considering that only three alignment options are available for graphics, it's remarkable how much variation exists among different sites on the Web. Web designers create varied appearances for their pages through the *types* of graphics they use. Where do these graphics come from? Here are a few possibilities:

- ❏ New images
- ❏ Text-manipulation programs
- ❏ Scanned photographs
- ❏ Stealing images off the Net

New images

If you're artistically inclined or want to use relatively straightforward graphics or icons, the easiest way to produce graphics for your Web pages is to create them yourself. A bewildering number of graphics applications are available for Windows, Mac, and UNIX users, at prices ranging from free to $50 to thousands of dollars for real top-notch stuff.

To give you an example, I created the opening graphic for the Dark Box (shown in Figure 8-2) from scratch in about 20 minutes. I used a commercial Mac program called Color It to produce the text and graphic and then translated the final output to GIF format with a separate shareware program called GraphicConverter.

I asked a couple of other Web designers who use cool graphics what tools they use to produce their images. Patti Siering, graphics designer for EuroGrafix (the Web page shown in Figure 8-12) told me that she used Adobe Photoshop 3 and Strata Studio Pro 1.5.1 to produce the image in Figure 8-12.

Figure 8-12: Cool EuroGrafix image.

Another cool Web site is Traveling Software, the maker of LapLink. Web designer David Geller indicated that he used Aldus Photostyler for Windows to create most of the graphics on the Traveling Software page, shown in Figure 8-13.

 tip   ■

You may want to visit a few of these sites yourself. The URL for Euro-Grafix is `http://www.eurografix.com/eurograf/welcome.htm`, and the URL for Traveling Software is `http://www.halcyon.com/travsoft/`.

Figure 8-13: Traveling Software's opening image.

Here are some of the more popular graphics packages for each platform:

☐ **Windows:** Among the many applications for developing graphics in Microsoft Windows are Illustrator, FreeHand, Painter, Fractal Design Dabbler, Canvas, Ray Dream Designer, SmartSketch, CorelDRAW!, MacroModel, AutoSketch, Kai's Power Tools, 3D Sketch, and Elastic Reality.

☐ **Macintosh:** Because it remains the premiere platform for graphics, you'll find that most graphics applications are available for the Mac. In addition to the "big three" — Adobe Photoshop, Aldus FreeHand, and Adobe Illustrator — you'll find Macintosh graphics programs such as Drawing Table, Color It, Specular Collage, KPT Bryce, Paint Alchemy, TextureScape, Painter, Kai's Power Tools, and Alias Sketch.

☐ **UNIX:** Fewer graphics programs are available for UNIX systems, but the programs that are available are quite powerful. Look for IslandDraw and IslandPaint, Photoshop, FusionArt, GINOGRAPH, Illustrator, Image Alchemy, Magic Inkwell, and Visual Reality.

Text-manipulation programs

I really like funky or interesting text effects in Web pages — not just simple things such as text in boxes, but shadows, textured letters, and twisted or wavy baselines. Look at the lettering in the Dark Box image earlier, in figure 8.3, to see the kind of thing that I think looks cool.

I manipulated the text in the Dark Box page the hard way, from within a general-purpose graphics editor. A smarter method would have been to use one of the many type-manipulation programs that are available. I have two favorites: Pixar Typestry (available for both Macs and PCs) and Broderbund TypeStyler (Mac only).

Typestry is astoundingly powerful, offering a staggering variety of options. Figure 8-14 shows a simple graphic produced in the program (it looks much better in color).

Figure 8-14: Text graphics in Typestry.

TypeStyler is easier to use and offers a more general-purpose graphics environment but lacks the sophistication of Typestry. As Figure 8-15 shows, the program enables you to produce attractive text for Web pages. The many graphics included with the HTML documents on the floppy disk in the back of this book were almost all done within TypeStyler.

Figure 8-15: Text graphics in TypeStyler.

Scanned photographs

Another way to produce graphics for your Web site is to use a scanner and work with existing art. If you're a photography buff, you probably have hundreds of original photographs from which you can glean cool additions for your site.

A few years ago, I was traveling in Paris and took what turned out to be a great photograph of the beautiful Sacré Coeur. A few minutes of work with a scanner made the photo instant artwork to include in my Web page, as shown in Figure 8-16.

Figure 8-16: Scanned image of Sacré Coeur.

Scanners offer further options for producing fun and interesting graphics. I also scanned the image shown in Figure 8-16 as black-and-white line art, producing the interesting abstract graphic in Figure 8-17.

If I were designing a Web site that I expected to attract users who have slow connections, I could use small black-and-white representations of art, each small image, or thumbnail image, as a button that produces the full color image, to save people time waiting for data that they may not want. The HTML could look like the following:

```
<A HREF="big-image.gif"><IMG SRC="little-image.gif"></A>
```

Figure 8-17: Sacré Coeur as line art.

> Thumbnail versions of large graphical images are common (and appreciated by just about everyone), so if you create a page that contains many pictures, think about minimizing the data transfer with smaller versions that refer to larger images.

Another difference between the images in Figures 8-16 and 8-17 is size. Figure 8-16 works on computers that have a palette of 256 colors (standard for GIF format), meaning that each pixel of information is represented in the data file by enough data to specify which of the 256 colors is needed at each point. Eight bits are used in this case, meaning that whereas the black-and-white version simply needs to specify "on" or "off" for each pixel (1 bit), the color version needs eight times as much information to display the information correctly. Trim the color palette on an image from 256 colors to, say, 16 (that is, from 8 bits of data per pixel to 4 bits of data per pixel), and you've lopped 50 percent off the size of your graphic, often without adverse effect on the image.

> Another way to work with scanners is to scan scrawls, doodles, or pictures that you create with pencils, pens, color markers, paint, pastels, or what have you, and then incorporate those objects into your Web page. Or get even more creative: scan in aluminum foil, crumpled tissues, your cat (note that this would be a "cat scan"), wood, a piece of clothing, or just about anything else.

■■■

Copyright laws are serious, and I strongly discourage you from scanning in images from any published work that is not in the public domain. The cover of Sports Illustrated might be terrific this week, but if you scan it in and display it in your Web page, you're asking for some very serious trouble.

If you're working with scanners, you already know about some of the best software tools available. I'll just note that I always use Photoshop when I'm working with color or gray scale scans.

Stealing images off the Net

There's another way to get images that doesn't involve being artistic or using a scanner: you can find interesting, attractive graphics online. Think of Net graphics as being virtual clip art (you can use real clip art, too), though don't forget that some of the images might be copyrighted. Just because MCI has a Web site (at `http://www.mci.com/`) doesn't mean that you can nip over and borrow its logo without permission!

To show you what's out there, I culled some icons from a couple of cool icon archives on the Web. Finding these icons was a long, tedious task, because many archives contain what I consider to be just plain ugly icons, but I couldn't tell until I loaded the entire page of icons on the screen.

Chris Stephens at Virginia Commonwealth University offers a terrific set of icons that even load quickly. Connect to the rather weird numeric URL `http://128.172.69.103/bullet.html`, and you'll see much more than the small portion of the set shown in Figure 8-18.

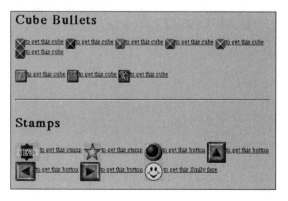

Figure 8-18: *Some of the icons in the Stephens archive.*

Another site that offers icons and graphics suitable for inclusion in your own pages is CERN, the Swiss physics lab where the World Wide Web was born (is it any wonder that CERN has all sorts of cool stuff on its server?). The URL for the CERN icon archive is `http://www.w3.org/hypertext/WWW/Icons/WWW`. See Figure 8-19.

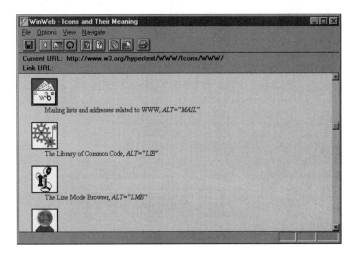

Figure 8-19: CERN icon library.

Cut out the middleman and get the master list of icon home pages by going to Yahoo (`http://www.yahoo.com/`) and looking in Computers ➪ World Wide Web ➪ Programming ➪ Icons.

Of course, you can just travel the Net and, when you see something you like, grab it with a screen capture program or download it directly. Different Web browsers offer different tools to accomplish just this task. With winWeb or MacWeb, for example, simply click on a graphic and hold the mouse button down, and suddenly there's a pop-up menu with the option of saving that graphic to the disk. If you take this route, however, be sensitive to possible copyright infringement.

Transparent Colors

One subtle thing that I did with graphics in this chapter was replace the background color around the edges of the image with a *transparent color* — one that allows the background color of the window to bleed through. Transparent colors (available only with GIF format images, as far as I know) almost instantly make pages look cooler. Of course, in this book, there *are* no colors.

Figure 8-20 shows two versions of the same icon. The graphic on the top hasn't had its white background set to transparent; the one on the bottom has. Some difference, eh?

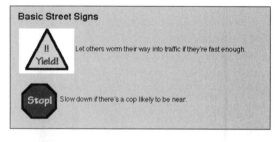

Figure 8-20: Transparent graphics.

Although very few of the major graphics or type-manipulation packages supports transparent GIFs (or GIFs at all, for that matter), a couple of simple shareware applications that are available on the Net enable you to choose a color for a specific graphic from the GIF color palette and set that color to be the transparent one.

For Windows users, the program of choice is GIFTRANS. You can obtain this program easily from the archive of the University of North Carolina at Chapel Hill; the URL is `ftp://sunsite.unc.edu/pub/packages/infosystems/WWW/tools/giftrans`.

On the Macintosh, the program Transparency, written by Aaron Giles, is rough and primitive but does the job admirably. You can get a copy of this program off the Net at `ftp://ftp.med.cornell.edu/pub/aarong/transparency/`.

If you're working on a UNIX box, or if you like working within the DOS environment, you can use GIFTool, which is available at `http://www.homepages.com/tools/`.

For a comprehensive list of utilities and all sorts of goodies, zip over to Yahoo (`http://www.yahoo.com/`) and look in Computers ⇨ World Wide Web ⇨ Programming.

Audio, Video, and other Media

Graphics definitely add pizazz to a Web site, but there are more media that you can use to develop your cool Web pages, including audio and video. Some significant limitations plague these add-on media, however, not the least of which is that they're not displayed or played within the Web browser, but require additional utility programs to work . . . utility programs that often are not included with standard Web browser distributions.

Audio fragments are probably the most fun — it's great to hear voices or music coming from your computer and they're quite easy to add to your own pages. The audio recordings are usually in what's called a micro-law (or you'll see this written as mu-law) format, and can be included as a button or hot spot just like any other URL. Here's an example:

```
You're invited to listen to <A HREF="audio.au">a sample of my latest
album</A>
```

Users that clicked on the phrase *a sample of my latest album* would then download an audio file (typically 75K or larger), and then a separate, external audio player program would be launched to actually play the audio clip. A simple audio clip is also included on the floppy disk in the back of this book.

Be careful when you're adding audio to your site, however; these files can grow incredibly quickly and become huge. A ten second audio clip can grow to over 150K, which could represent *quite* a long download period for people accessing the Web via slow dialup connections.

Multimedia PCs and AV Macintosh have a variety of built-in audio capabilities, including the ability to record audio directly from an attached microphone. Save the file that's produced and ensure it has a .WAV filename suffix. My personal favorite for recording and editing audio is a great shareware program called Wham. You can learn about this, and many other audio tools by checking in at Yahoo at `http://www.yahoo.com/Computers/World_Wide_Web/Programming`.

Movies are found in two formats, QuickTime and MPEG (Motion Picture Experts Group) format. MPEG is the format of choice for the Web, however, since it's the most universal, with MPEG players available for Mac, PC, and Unix systems.

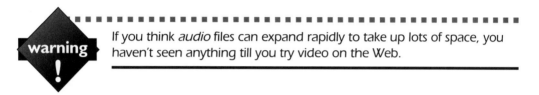

warning !

If you think *audio* files can expand rapidly to take up lots of space, you haven't seen anything till you try video on the Web.

The format for including an MPEG sequence is simple:

```
The latest <A HREF="video.mpeg">Music Video</A> is finally here!
```

The Web browsers see the filename suffix .PEG and then know to download the file specified and launch an external video player program.

You can learn a lot more about working with MPEG and other video formats, and sneak a peek at some public domain video and animation archive sites, by popping over to Yahoo. Check out `http://www.yahoo.com/Computers/Multimedia/Video` there.

I could say lots more about the fun and frustration of working with graphics and other media in Web pages. One thing's for sure: however people accomplish the task, you'll see a million very cool graphics, icons, buttons, separator bars, and other gizmos all over the Web. Keep a skeptical eye on your own work, though, to make sure that your neat doodads don't overtake the theme and message of your site.

In my view, at least, cool Web pages are those that intelligently incorporate their graphics into the overall design and that don't fall apart or become unusable (or otherwise frustrating) when users don't or can't load the graphics, ending up with ALT=text information instead. In the next chapter, you learn about the slick layout and formatting options the Netscape Navigator Web browser offers. The Netscape features may not be standard — yet — but they enable you to create even cooler Web pages.

The Netscape HTML Extensions

The different World Wide Web browser programs understood the same HTML formatting tags until Netscape Navigator showed up late in 1994. Netscape Communications Corporation, the folks who make Netscape, added some extensions — extra formatting tags that Netscape Navigator supports — to HTML 1.0. At the time of this writing, only Netscape Navigator supports the formatting tags discussed here. This chapter introduces some of the coolest added features.

In this chapter

- ❏ Netscape Navigator's history
- ❏ Centering and more horizontal rules
- ❏ List improvements
- ❏ Character manipulation
- ❏ Refined image-placement options

If you've read the whole book up to this point, you know all there is to know about HTML coding. Well, almost. This chapter focuses on a set of nonstandard extensions that are understood only by the Netscape Navigator program, sometimes referred to simply as Netscape. As you'll learn, the Netscape extensions are terrifically useful and offer the capability to create far cooler pages than you can using only standard HTML 1.0 tags. (The final chapter in this book briefly discusses various advanced capabilities that are part of standard HTML.)

The good news is that almost all the Netscape extensions will be included in HTML 3.0, which is expected to be released sometime in 1995. Perhaps by the end of 1995, all Web browsers will understand and correctly process the Netscape tags.

Netscape Navigator's History

Nothing has been more influential in expanding the popularity of the World Wide Web than Mosaic, a piece of software developed at the NCSA (National Center for Supercomputing Applications) located at the University of Illinois, Urbana-Champaign. With a team of Mac and PC programmers, NCSA created several invaluable Internet and networking utilities (all free), including NCSA Telnet and NCSA Mosaic.

Released for UNIX, Macintosh, and Microsoft Windows, Mosaic offered a unified graphical environment for reading documents created for a relatively obscure Swiss network documentation system called the World Wide Web. And suddenly, it seemed that everyone and her brother was on the Web, reading and creating Web documents, and having a fabulous time.

The key programmer, a young chap named Marc Andreessen, was contacted by industry visionary Jim Clark, the founder of Silicon Graphics, about creating a commercial venture that would expand Mosaic and be on the cutting edge of Web-server design, Web commerce, and other vital underlying technologies. Marc signed up, and Mosaic Communications was born.

As one of the creators of Mosaic, Andreessen was intimately familiar with HTML and with the design tradeoffs within NCSA Mosaic. He was determined not to make the same compromises with the new browser. The good news for all of us is that he wasn't constrained and created Netscape Navigator, a much more powerful Web browser program.

The Netscape extensions are expected to be part of HTML 3.0. Today, however, if you write Web documents that contain the Netscape extensions, only people who are using Netscape Navigator will see the documents that you design. Everyone else will see something similar, but not exactly the same.

And there's the rub: should you design your cool Web pages for all browsers or for the Netscape user, or do you wrestle with trying to combine the two in a single design? I talk about that dilemma throughout this chapter, showing you how I tried to avoid the greater dangers.

Centering and More Horizontal Rules

Of the many additions to the hypertext markup language that are introduced in Netscape, the one that I like most is `<CENTER>`, with its partner tag `</CENTER>`. Any information between the two tags is centered on the screen of the browser. This extension is particularly useful for opening graphics, but as you begin to design more complex pages, you probably will find other places where it can be a great help.

One situation in which using `<CENTER>` is a big win is centering the headline or title of a text HTML page. Remember the enchilada sauce recipe from Chapter 5? The following example shows how the text could be enhanced for Netscape:

```
<HTML>
<HEAD>
<TITLE>Dave's Enchilada Sauce</TITLE>
<!- written with Netscape extensions ->
</HEAD><BODY>
<CENTER>
<B>Dave's Enchilada Sauce</B><BR>
<I>guaranteed to enhance any enchilada!</I>
</CENTER>
<OL>
<LI>Heat a large sauce pan and saut&egrave; until soft:
<UL>
<LI>Two tablespoons virgin olive oil
<LI>A large onion, chopped
</UL>
<LI>Sprinkle in a quarter cup of flour.<BR>
<LI>Jazz it up by adding:
<UL>
<LI>Two tablespoons of chili powder
<LI>Two teaspoons of cumin
<LI>One teaspoon of garlic powder
</UL>
<LI>Mix in a quart of water.
<LI>Finally, add a teaspoon of salt if desired.
</OL>
Whisk as sauce thickens then simmer for 20 minutes.
</BODY>
</HTML>
```

Figure 9-1 shows how the preceding recipe would look in Netscape. The recipe is more visually interesting but still rather boring. As you go through this chapter, you'll learn about some enhancements that can make this text much more attractive.

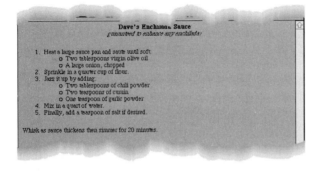

Figure 9-1: Centered text in Netscape Navigator.

Horizontal rules are helpful, but let's be honest: a uniform line across the screen can get *boring*. The Netscape gang also thought horizontal rules were boring, so they extended the <HR> command with some additions (perhaps too many): SIZE, WIDTH, ALIGN, and NOSHADE. The first three of these options take values.

SIZE enables you to specify the height of the horizontal line, in pixels. Want the slimmest line possible? Try using <HR SIZE=1> in your document.

A pixel is a single dot on a computer screen. A horizontal line that is 1 pixel high, therefore, is the tiniest line possible. Your screen probably has about 500 horizontal rows of pixels. SIZE=1 specifies a single pixel-high line.

WIDTH can be specified either in absolute pixels (a typical screen probably is 600 to 800 pixels wide) or in a percentage of the screen width. If you want a horizontal rule that is exactly 75 percent of the width of the current viewing window, you could use <HR WIDTH=75%> as your HTML sequence.

Because you can have lines that don't extend over the entire width of the browser, Netscape enables you to specify where you want a line snippet to be placed. Just as you can with the ALIGN options for images, you can specify that horizontal lines be placed LEFT, CENTER, or RIGHT. To have a line that's half the width of the browser window and centered, you would use <HR WIDTH=50% ALIGN=CENTER>.

Finally, close examination of the horizontal lines displayed in Netscape shows that the lines are shaded to offer a quasi-three-dimensional appearance. If you really want a solid black bar, use the NOSHADE option.

You can combine these options in fun and interesting ways, as in the following example:

```
<CENTER><B>A Visit to the Pyramids!</B></CENTER><P>
<HR SIZE=3 WIDTH=5%>
<HR SIZE=3 WIDTH=10%>
<HR SIZE=3 WIDTH=20%>
<HR SIZE=3 WIDTH=30%>
<HR SIZE=3 WIDTH=40%>
<HR SIZE=3 WIDTH=50%>
<HR SIZE=3 WIDTH=60%>
<HR SIZE=3 WIDTH=100% NOSHADE>
```

This kind of detail can get complex, but the result can be pretty cool, as shown in Figure 9-2.

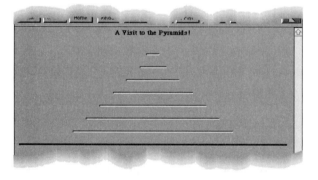

Figure 9-2: A pyramid, one line at a time.

What does the Web page in Figure 9-2 look like if you view it in a different browser? Figure 9-3 tells the story.

Figure 9-3: Not much of a pyramid in MacWeb.

And that's the danger, in a nutshell: you may design a wickedly cool Web page with the Netscape extensions, but seen from other browsers, your page looks like you used the Paste command too many times (or worse). In this particular case, therefore, I recommend that you use horizontal lines sparingly and in the default style (standard height, 100 percent width).

List Improvements

HTML lists have three basic extensions: one for ordered lists (<OL>), one for unordered lists (<UL>), and one for individual list items (<LI>).

Standard ordered lists have no options. You specify that you have an ordered list, and the list items are displayed with incremented numeric values: step 1, step 2, step 3, and so on. If you're creating a multilevel outline or other multilevel list, however, different forms of notation for the different levels can be quite useful. You may use A to Z for the highest level, numbers for the second level, and a to z for the lowest level. That format is, of course, the typical outline format, taught in English class, and an example of it looks like the following:

A. Introduction

    1. Title

        a. Author

        b. Institution

        c. Working title (20 words or fewer)

    2. Justification for research

        a. What? Why?

    3. Findings

    4. Conclusions

B. Body of Paper

    1. Previous research

    2. Research methods used

    3. Results and findings

C. Conclusion

    1. Implications

    2. Directions for future research

D. References

If you were to try to reproduce the preceding example within HTML, the best you could do with standard HTML notation would be to have three levels of numbered-list items, many bullet points, or no indentation at all. None of those options is what you want, naturally, and that's where the Netscape ordered-list extensions come in handy.

Ordered lists have two extensions: TYPE, which specifies the numeric type to use; and START, which begins the count at a number other than the default (default is 1). You can use five types of counting values:

- ❑ TYPE=A is uppercase alphabetic (A, B, C, D).
- ❑ TYPE=a is lowercase alphabetic (a, b, c, d).
- ❑ TYPE=I is uppercase Roman numerals (I, II, III, IV).
- ❑ TYPE=i is lowercase Roman numerals (i, ii, iii, iv).
- ❑ TYPE=1 (the default) is Arabic numerals (1, 2, 3, 4).

To have an ordered list begin with the fourth Roman numeral in uppercase, you could use <OL TYPE=I START=4>. The default for a list is <OL TYPE=1 START=1>.

If you've been experimenting with Netscape, you may already have found that different levels of unordered lists produce differently shaped bullets. In fact, Netscape supports three types of bullets — a solid disc, a circle, and a square — and you can specify which should be used for your unordered list with TYPE. For example, do you want a list in which every item is tagged with a square? <UL TYPE=square> does the trick.

Within the <LI> tag, you can specify TYPE=shape (if you're in the middle of an unordered list) or START=value (to change the current count for an ordered list). The following example shows how some of these features can be used in a Web document:

```
<B>Geometric Ramblings</B>
<OL TYPE=1>
<LI>Facets of a square:
<UL TYPE=square>
<LI>Four sides of equal length
</UL>
<LI>Interesting facts about circles:
<UL TYPE=disc>
<LI>Maximum enclosed area, shortest line
</UL>
</OL>
<CENTER>Weird, unrelated information.</CENTER>
<OL TYPE=1>
<LI VALUE=3> And much, much more!
</OL>
```

Figure 9-4 shows how the preceding HTML text would be presented to the user in Netscape. Note particularly that the numbered list seems to flow without any interruption, something that would be impossible to accomplish without the Netscape addition to the ordered list.

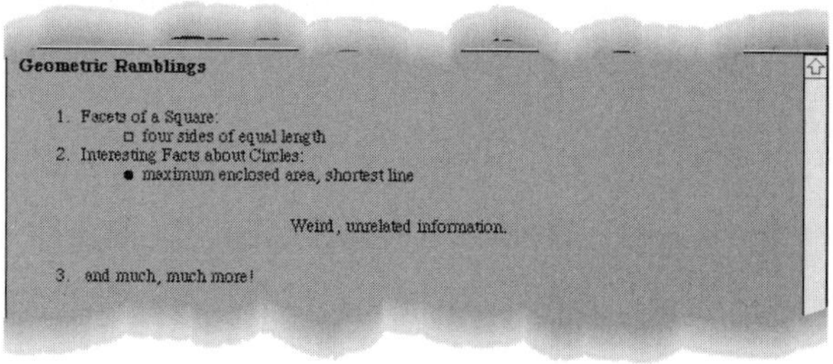

Figure 9-4: Geometric ramblings in Netscape.

Character Manipulation

One of the most tedious aspects of working within the confines of standard HTML is that any time you want to present information at a size larger than the default, you have to specify a header of some sort. But because headers have special formatting associated with them, including adding line breaks, they can ruin your design.

The Netscape folks recognized the "size" problem and added a couple of much-needed font-manipulation commands. To change the default size of the font in your document, for example, use the <BASEFONT> tag and its required argument SIZE=n, in which n is a typeface size that varies from system to system, based on the user's configuration options. The range of possible size values is 1 to 7; the default font size is 3.

To change a specific word or phrase, you can use the other new text size tag: <FONT SIZE=n>. Again, the size that you specify must be between 1 and 7, though you can also use relative size changes with "+n" or "-n", so long as the resultant font size is in the range of 1-7. The <FONT SIZE=n> feature is a *very* cool addition to HTML that can jazz up a page instantly. All font size changes should end with either </FONT> or another <FONT SIZE=n> that restores the text to the desired size. Consider the following enchilada recipe I can create now:

```
<HTML>
<HEAD>
<TITLE>Dave's Enchilada Sauce</TITLE>
<!- written with Netscape extensions ->
</HEAD><BODY>
<BASEFONT SIZE=+1>  <!- make all text a bit bigger ->
<CENTER>
<FONT SIZE=6><B>Dave's Enchilada Sauce</B><BR>
<FONT SIZE=4><I>guaranteed to enhance any enchilada!</I>
<FONT SIZE=3>
<HR SIZE=4 WIDTH=70% ALIGN=CENTER>
</CENTER>
<BLOCKQUOTE>
I was first introduced to this recipe while visiting a friend in Chula
Vista, a predominantly Mexican area of San Diego. Her mother was a
fabulous cook (with tamales to die for!) and she shared her simplified
'gringo' enchilada recipe with me, a recipe that has evolved into...
</BLOCKQUOTE>
<OL>
<LI>Heat a large sauce pan and saute until soft:
<UL>
<LI>Two tablespoons <FONT SIZE=+1>virgin olive oil</FONT>.
<LI>A large <FONT SIZE=+1>onion</FONT>, chopped.
</UL>
<LI>Sprinkle in a quarter cup of <FONT SIZE=+1>flour</FONT>.
<LI>Mix in a quart of <FONT SIZE=+1>water</FONT>.
<LI>Add a teaspoon of <FONT SIZE=+1>salt</FONT> if desired.
</OL>
<FONT SIZE=+1>Jazz it up by adding:</FONT>
<UL>
<LI>Two tablespoons of <FONT SIZE=+1>chili powder</FONT>
<LI>Two teaspoons of <FONT SIZE=+1>cumin</FONT>
<LI>One teaspoon of <FONT SIZE=+1>garlic powder</FONT>
</UL>
Whisk as sauce thickens then simmer for 20 minutes.
</BODY>
</HTML>
```

Here, the HTML code gets complex. It's difficult to edit this recipe and keep track of what is formatting and what is text. Figure 9-5 shows this version of the enchilada-sauce recipe in Netscape.

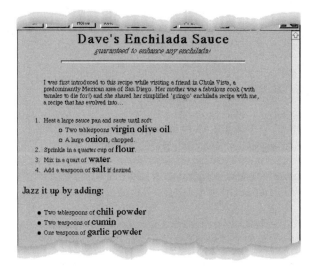

Figure 9-5: Another try at the enchilada sauce recipe.

The `<BLOCKQUOTE>` formatting tag is the standard way to indent quoted material within an HTML document and it's part of standard HTML too. As you can see in Figure 9-5, this tag creates a block indent of a paragraph.

Another feature that Netscape offers for text formatting in Web documents is cumulative formatting capability. Suppose that you specify the following in a non-Netscape Web browser:

```
<B><I>This should be in italicized bold</I></B>
```

What would happen? The result would be a sentence in italics, with the bold formatting lost.

But in Netscape, it's a different story. Netscape fixes the "lost attribute" problem by enabling you to accumulate formatting options as your heart desires. If you want to have a word in bold italics, a little larger than the other text, and in a monospace font, try the following:

```
<B><I><FONT SIZE=+1><TT>emphasis!</TT></FONT></I></B>
```

Refined Image-Placement Options

Chapter 8 explored the creation and placement of graphics in Web documents, but it was clear that some capabilities were still missing. Most frustrating for burgeoning Web designers is the lack of true text wrapping around graphics. Standard HTML merely allows you to have a single line of text adjacent to a graphic and aligned with the top of the image, the middle of the image, or the bottom.

Perhaps the *most* exciting improvement to HTML 1.0 offered in Netscape is an extended set of image-placement options. Table 9-1 summarizes the new alignment options in Netscape.

Table 9-1	Netscape Image-Alignment Options
Option	**Meaning**
LEFT	Float image; fill text to the right of graphic
RIGHT	Float image; fill text to the left of graphic
TOP	Same as old HTML ALIGN=top
TEXTTOP	Align graphic with the top of the tallest text in the line
MIDDLE	Same as old HTML ALIGN=middle
ABSMIDDLE	Align middle of text with middle of graphic
BASELINE	Synonymous with ALIGN=bottom
BOTTOM	Same as old HTML ALIGN=bottom
ABSBOTTOM	Align bottom of image with bottom of line

Although the Netscape image alignment options offer much more control, they also make formatting more confusing. Some of the new alignment options are in fact synonyms of earlier options, which can be quite puzzling.

That aside, I'll try to make sense of all the options for you, because the options really *are* terrific. The first thing to remember is that whatever you design with these extensions still must look attractive and interesting to people who are using other Web browsers besides Netscape; unless you remain committed to that goal, your cool page in Netscape could easily look like a barely formatted mess in winWeb or Mosaic.

tip

For that reason, I recommend that you skip the subtle refinements of the TEXTTOP, ABSMIDDLE, and ABSBOTTOM alignment options. These options are so close to the standard TOP, MIDDLE, and BOTTOM alignments that it's better to stick with the standard alignments to make your page more universally meaningful.

After jettisoning the TEXTTOP, ABSMIDDLE, and ABSBOTTOM alignment options, the list is pared down to a more manageable pair of alignment options: left and right. These options are better demonstrated than discussed. The following example uses both options:

```
<B>Generic File Icon</B><BR>
<IMG SRC="generic-file.gif" ALIGN=left>
This is a generic file — that is, one that doesn't have any
application ownership information stored in the Mac file system or
its own resource fork. Opening these files typically results in the use
of the
<B>TeachText</B> or <B>SimpleText</B> application, if
possible, although you can fine-tune that with the new
<B>Easy Launch</B> control panel.
<P>
<B>Generic Folder Icon</B><BR>
<IMG SRC="generic-folder.gif" ALIGN=right>
This is a standard folder icon on the Macintosh. Folders can
contain just about anything, including files, applications,
and other folders. Opening a folder results in the display
of the contents of that folder in a separate window on
the Macintosh.
```

Figure 9-6 shows how the preceding text is formatted within Netscape — quite a step up from the primitive placement options you learned about in Chapter 8!

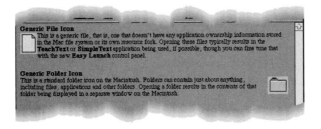

Figure 9-6: Floating graphics in Netscape.

Because other World Wide Web browsers (all except Netscape) don't recognize the Netscape alignment options, it's always valuable to nip into one of those browsers to see how things are presented to the reader. Figure 9-7 shows the same HTML code that produced Figure 9-6, but from within MacWeb. Notice that the design of the HTML code — particularly the use of the boldface section title before the graphic and text — results in a dramatically different yet attractive appearance.

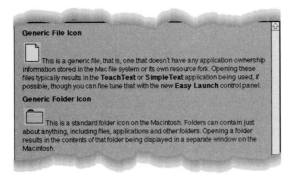

Figure 9-7: Floating graphics in MacWeb.

Further options have been added to the now complex <IMG> formatting tag in Netscape. One new option enables you to specify the WIDTH and HEIGHT of the graphic when the graphic is loaded, which allows acceleration of the display of the document while the graphics are being loaded. Values are specified in pixels, as follows:

```
<IMG SRC="windows.gif" WIDTH=200 HEIGHT=350>
```

The preceding example would reserve a 200-by-350-pixel box on-screen for the graphic, which would be loaded in full after the text so that the reader can begin reading the text right away.

The BORDER variable can be used to great effect; it allows you to specify the exact width of the border around an image. The BORDER option is particularly useful if your graphic is also a hot link or anchor. The following shows an example:

```
<!- Tic-Tac-Toe ->
<CENTER>
<FONT SIZE=+3><B>Tic-Tac-Toe</B><FONT SIZE=+1><BR>
It's X's Turn... (<A HREF="">This color</A> indicates a recommended move)
<P>
<A HREF="topleft"><IMG SRC='box+x.gif' BORDER=0></A>
<A HREF="topcntr"><IMG SRC="box.gif" BORDER=0></A>
<A HREF="topright"><IMG SRC="box.gif" BORDER=0></A>
<BR>
<A HREF="left"><IMG SRC="box+o.gif" BORDER=0></A>
<A HREF="center"><IMG SRC="box+o.gif" BORDER=0></A>
<A HREF="right"><IMG SRC="box.gif" BORDER=2></A>
<BR>
<A HREF="btmleft"><IMG SRC="box+x.gif" BORDER=0></A>
<A HREF="btmcenter"><IMG SRC="box.gif" BORDER=0></A>
<A HREF="btmright"><IMG SRC="box.gif" BORDER=0></A>
</CENTER>
```

The resulting graphic is displayed in Figures 9-8 and 9-9 within Netscape and MacWeb, respectively. Notice that the BORDER specification allows me to indicate the recommended next move in Netscape simply by placing a blue (or grey, for our figures in this book!) border around the box. That information is missing in the MacWeb figure (Figure 9-9).

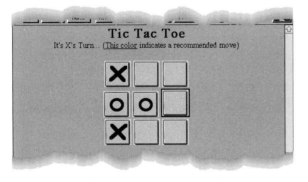

Figure 9-8: Tic-tac-toe in Netscape Navigator.

I cheated a little on the HTML listing for Figures 9-8 and 9-9. Look at how I managed to get the phrase *This color* to show up in the appropriate color for a hotlink in the browser — a null hypertext reference. This is much clearer if you look at the HTML example listing on the included floppy disk with Netscape Navigator.

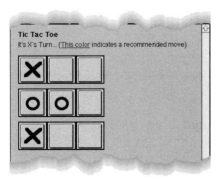

Figure 9-9: Tic-tac-toe in MacWeb.

Two additions that I think are more useful for image alignment are the VSPACE and HSPACE options, which control the vertical and horizontal space around each graphic. Consider an example of left and right alignment. When displayed, the text started at a different distance from the left margin, based on the width of the graphic. With HSPACE I can fix this problem by specifying a different number of pixels as a horizontal buffer between the graphics and the text adjacent, as follows:

```
<B>Generic File Icon</b><br>
<IMG SRC="generic-file.gif" ALIGN=left HSPACE=12>
This is a generic file, that is, one that doesn't have
any application ownership information stored in the
Mac file system or its own resource fork. Opening
these files typically results in the <b>TeachText</b>
or <b>SimpleText</b> application being used, if possible,
though you can fine tune that with the new
<b>Easy Launch</b> control panel.
<p>
```

(continued)

```
<B>Generic Folder Icon</b><br>
<IMG SRC="generic-folder.gif" ALIGN=left HSPACE=10>
This is a standard folder icon on the Macintosh.
Folders can contain just about anything, including
files, applications and other folders. Opening a folder
results in the contents of that folder being displayed
in a separate window on the Macintosh.
```

Figure 9-10 demonstrates the result of the preceding text.

Figure 9-10: HSPACE corrects the graphic alignment.

At this point, you're learning to have some real control of the display of the document and can begin to design some cool Web pages. But I need to mention one more formatting addition before you go wild with the various Netscape extensions to HTML.

If you experiment, you'll find that if you're wrapping text around a large graphic, <BR> simply moves to the next line in the wrapped area. That effect is *not* always what you want. To break the line and move back to the margin, past the graphics, use <BR CLEAR=left> to move to the left margin, <BR CLEAR=right> to move down to a clear right margin, or <BR CLEAR=all> to move down until both margins are clear of the image.

Tossing all the additions into the mix, here's the final version of the Macintosh icon tutorial:

```
<HTML>
<HEAD>
<TITLE>An Introduction to Mac Icons</TITLE>
<BASEFONT SIZE=+2>
</HEAD><BODY>
<CENTER>
```

(continued)

(continued)

```
<FONT SIZE=+2><B>Intro to Macintosh Icons</B><BR>
<FONT SIZE=-1><I>Some of these are System 7.x only</I>
<FONT SIZE=-1>
</CENTER>
<P>
<B>Generic File Icon</B><BR>
<IMG SRC="generic-file.gif" ALIGN=left HSPACE=18 VSPACE=8>
This is a generic file — that is, one that doesn't have
any application ownership information stored in the Mac
file system or its own resource fork. Opening
these files typically results in the use of the <B>TeachText</B>
or <B>SimpleText</B> application, if
possible, although you can fine-tune that with the new
<B>Easy Launch</B> control panel.
<P>
<B>Generic Folder Icon</B><BR>
<IMG SRC="generic-folder.gif" ALIGN=left HSPACE=15 VSPACE=6>
This is a standard folder icon on the Macintosh. Folders can
 contain just about anything, including files,
applications, and other folders. Opening a folder results
in the display of the contents of that folder in a
separate window on the Macintosh.
<P>
<B>System Folder Icon</B><BR>
<IMG SRC="system-folder.gif" ALIGN=left HSPACE=15 VSPACE=11>
A special folder at the top level of each hard disk
on the Macintosh is the <I>System Folder</I>. This folder
contains all the files, applications, and information
needed to run and maintain the Macintosh operating
system and all the goodies therein. The tiny Mac
icon inside the folder indicates that this
particular <I>System Folder</I> is <I>live</I> and that
the information inside was used to start
the current Macintosh.
<P>
Many files are located in the
<B>System Folder</B>, including the following:
<P>
<B>Apple Menu Icon</B><BR>
<IMG SRC="apple-menu.gif" ALIGN=left HSPACE=15 VSPACE=8>
Ever wondered where all the information that shows up on
the Apple menu (the menu you get when you click on
the <IMG SRC="apple-icon.gif"> in the top
```

(continued)

```
left corner of the menu bar)? They're all just
files, folders, applications and aliases tucked into
the Apple folder itself. Open this folder some time
and compare the contents with the results of clicking
on the Apple icon itself.
</BODY>
</HTML>
```

Figure 9-11 shows the result.

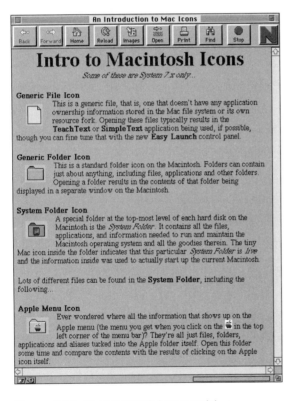

Figure 9-11: The Macintosh icon tutorial.

This chapter gave you a whirlwind tour of the many fascinating, helpful, and occasionally confusing extensions to HTML added by the team at Netscape Communications to the Netscape Navigator program. The next chapter explores the many search tools and Web-search databases on the World Wide Web. Chapter 10 discusses how to best design HTML documents that are not only cool and interesting, but also easy to index and easy for users to find.

Searching, Finding, and Being Found

This chapter discusses how Web search engines work and how to design your material so that it will be useful when indexed by WebCrawler, Lycos, Yahoo, and the many other search applications available on the Web. I also talk about how to get your Web pages included in the major Web indexes.

In this chapter

Having your own Web information is definitely cool, but like an exhibit of art in a gallery, the real fun begins when people come to visit. The fundamental puzzle of the World Wide Web — and the Internet as a whole — is *how to find information.* If *you* can't find stuff, it stands to reason that others will have difficulty finding your stuff too.

People have applied many different strategies for solving the indexing problem, ranging from creating simple databases of Web sites to which you submit information about your site to unleashing powerful *crawler* programs that stealthily visit your site and add your information to their massive indexes.

Visiting Some Web-Site Catalogs

Millions of documents are available on the World Wide Web, but a comparatively small number of sites offer help in finding particular information. Not simply a list of favorite links, search sites are usually concerted team efforts to index the information on the Web and thereby increase the value of the Web as a publishing medium (rather than just a spot for random surfing).

Chief among those sites is the vastly popular Yahoo service, a database of more than 30,000 Web sites. EINet Galaxy and CUI W3 Catalog also are important Web-server database sites. And in terms of futuristic intrigue, both Lycos and the WebCrawler are fascinating attempts to index the ever-growing World Wide Web.

Yahoo

http://www.yahoo.com/

Of the many sites on the Web that offer comprehensive databases of other Web sites, my favorite is Yahoo, maintained by David Filo and Jerry Yang. Filo and Yang developed Yahoo while at Stanford University as a mechanism for maintaining their own ever-growing list of cool Web sites, and the site has grown so fast that their two UNIX servers couldn't keep up with the load. Today Yahoo has spun off as a separate business on a new, even faster system and has more than 40,000 Web sites indexed. See Figure 10-1 for the Yahoo home page.

To search for specific information in the Yahoo database, you click the search option in the menu bar. (In the figure, this option appears in the document instead of the menu bar. When this book was being written, the Yahoo folks were trying to deal with its incredible popularity by cutting back on its use of graphics.) The Yahoo search window is shown in Figure 10-2.

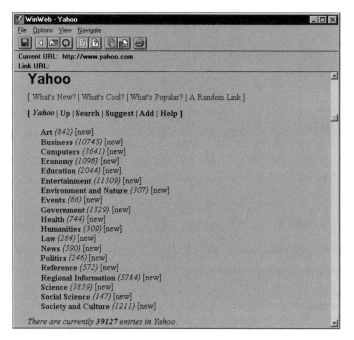

Figure 10-1: Yahoo home page.

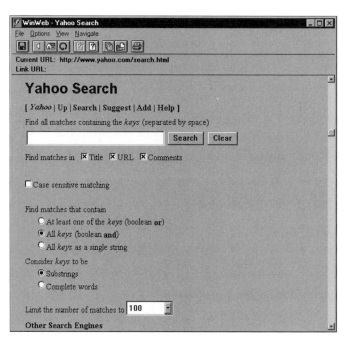

Figure 10-2: Searching for information in Yahoo.

I really enjoy puzzles and puzzle games, so I decided to add to my own home page a list of neat puzzle-related spots on the Web. I figure that I'll eventually want to be found when people search on *puzzle*. To search for puzzle-related information at Yahoo, enter **puzzle** in the search box and then click Search. The search results in 23 *hits* (matches) in the database of more than 30,000 indexed Web sites, as shown in Figure 10-3.

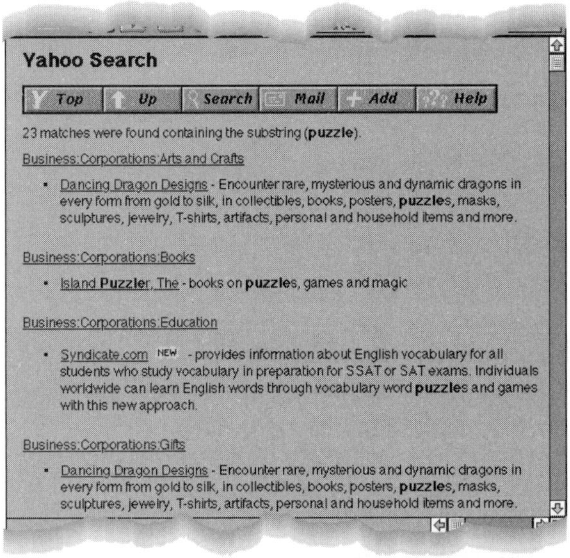

Figure 10-3: Puzzle sites on the Web.

Lycos

http://lycos.cs.cmu.edu/

Taking a very different approach to the problem, the Lycos site at Carnegie-Mellon University indexes more than two million Web documents by building a database of URLs and the first few lines of description from each Web page. Minimal textual information is included for the sites in the database, but the results still are surprisingly good. Figure 10-4 shows the cool Lycos home page:

Figure 10-4: Lycos home page, undeniably cool.

To allow comparison with Yahoo, I search Lycos for Web sites that have something to do with puzzles. Figure 10-5 shows the Lycos search screen. You'll notice immediately that there is no Search button. The Carnegie-Mellon team instead designed this page so that pressing the Enter or Return key on your keyboard submits the query. Indeed, any page that only has a single input box lets you omit the 'submit' or 'search' button.

Figure 10-5: Searching for puzzles in Lycos.

The search finds nearly a thousand puzzle-related sites in the Lycos database. Figure 10-6 shows the top 10 matches.

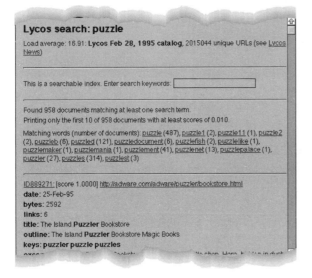

Figure 10-6: Puzzle sites found in Lycos.

The results in Lycos are puzzling (pardon the pun), and the format is one that only a computer person could love. Instead of just showing the matches, Lycos shows various statistical information, too. For example, you can see that the load on the system was 16.91; that it was using the 28 February 1995 catalog, with 2.015 million URLs; and that it found 958 matching documents (although only the first 10 were listed). The search engine is called Pursuit, and, similar to the more popular WAIS (Wide Area Information System) system, it offers relevance ratings, ranging from 1.000 (highest) down to 0.0001 (lowest). The first match — with ID889271 — has a perfect relevance score, as you can see.

Figure 10-7 shows the same Lycos results page you saw in Figure 10-6, only this time it's scrolled down so that you can see the entire entry for the Island Puzzler Bookstore.

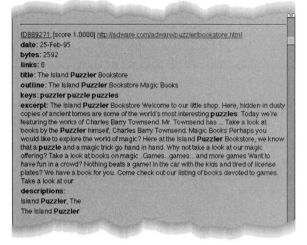

Figure 10-7: The Island Puzzler match in Lycos.

The text extracted from the Island Puzzler site offers a clue about how you can organize your own pages to ensure that relevant Lycos searches match your Web documents. Figure 10-8 shows the home page for the Island Puzzler, at `http://adware.com/adware/puzzler/bookstore.html`. Compare the prose listed in Figure 10-8 with the text included in the Lycos database in Figure 10-7.

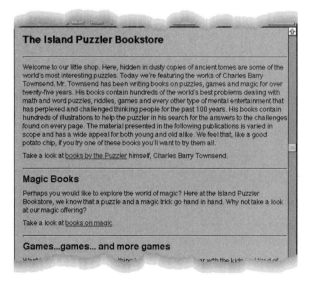

Figure 10-8: The Island Puzzler home page.

tip ■

> The first paragraph or two of information in your Web page should describe the contents of your Web site. Be sure to include common keywords and synonyms.

Instead of starting your page with some sexy graphics (which can't be indexed, of course), you may want to use a design like the following:

```
<HTML>
<HEAD>
<TITLE>The Mac WWW Reference Spot</TITLE>
</HEAD><BODY>
<IMG SRC="web-reference.gif" ALT="[opening graphic]">
<H1>The Mac World Wide Web Reference Spot</H1>
The one place to learn about creating HTML (hypertext
markup language), GIF and JPEG graphics (including
where to get cool graphics editors and translators),
HTTP servers, and a variety of other software and
sources that you'll need to create a way-cool Web spot
on your Macintosh. Don't forget — we also have some
of the slickest Web sites you can find on the Net
as potential inspiration for your own design!
```

Many keywords are stuffed into the preceding introduction, so people who are searching Lycos for keywords like *GIF* or *HTTP* would find the WWW Reference Spot page, and even people who are searching for *inspiration* have somewhere to go!

WebCrawler

http://webcrawler.cs.washington.edu/WebCrawler/WebQuery.html

Similar to Lycos, WebCrawler wanders about the Web autonomously, indexing entire Web documents in its copious database, filtering them through the WAIS search engine, and producing the results (with relevance ratings).

Searching in WebCrawler is simple. Continuing the theme of puzzles, I choose the search option, resulting in the screen shown in Figure 10-9.

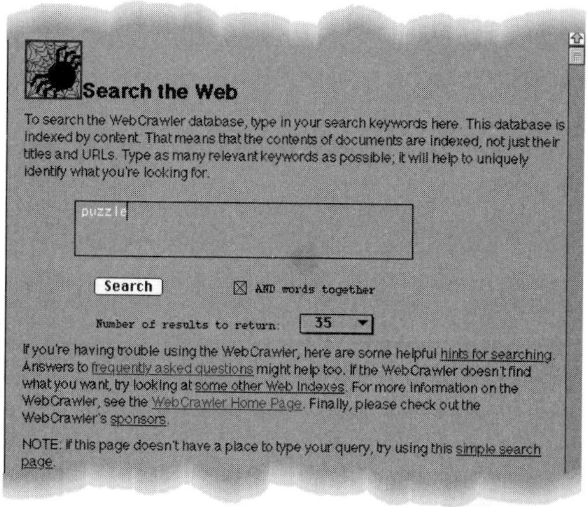

Figure 10-9: Searching in WebCrawler.

A search for *puzzle* probably is going to generate a ton of matches — but what the heck, right? If you type **puzzle**, you find that only 224 matches are produced — which is quite surprising, because Lycos found nearly a thousand. A good reason to search for information across multiple Web search sites, rather than just one. Perhaps more interesting, the Island Puzzler was proposed in Lycos as being the most relevant document, but in WebCrawler, it's barely in the top 10. Sorted by relevance, and with a relevance rating of 163 out of 1000, the Island Puzzler is only barely relevant to my search, according to WebCrawler. See Figure 10-10.

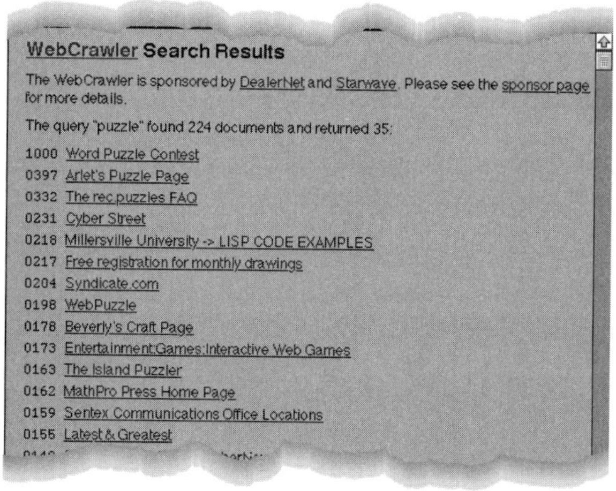

Figure 10-10: Result of searching for "puzzle".

Notice in Figure 10-10 that only the *titles* of the pages are listed, so there's no way for me to figure out why Cyber Street is ranked number 4, even though the title seems to have very little to do with puzzles.

EINet Galaxy

http://www.einet.net/

The EINet Galaxy is a Web site that is quite similar to Yahoo, albeit more rigidly organized. EINet Galaxy also is a bit more puzzling to use, as you can see from the opening page, shown in Figure 10-11.

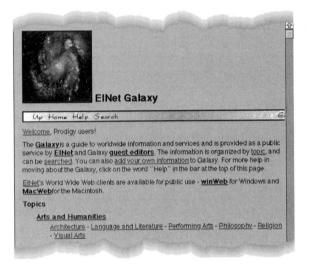

Figure 10-11: EINet Galaxy.

A search for information in EINet Galaxy produces a huge list of places that you can try searching, as shown in Figure 10-12. An actual search input box is tucked in at the very bottom of the page.

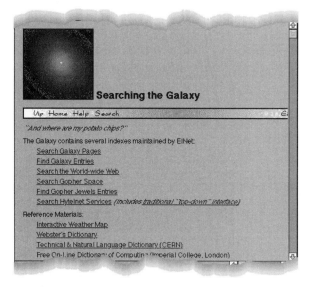

Figure 10-12: Searching in ElNet Galaxy.

Foolish consistency being the hobgoblin of little minds and helpful book examples, I opt to continue searching for puzzles, this time in the ElNet Galaxy search section. Again, the results are filtered through a WAIS engine; but this time, only five documents are matched (see Figure 10-13). A subtle mistake on my part: the default search is only for ElNet local documents. Click on the "World Wide Web (full text)" option and the search now returns 33 documents.

Figure 10-13: Puzzling results in ElNet Galaxy.

The result, unfortunately, demonstrates a few uncool Web design principles. For example, what is No Title, the fourth match in the list? This page also lacks meaningful navigational buttons or items other than those that lead me farther away from the Galaxy pages. A strip at the bottom that contains the options About ElNet Galaxy, Refine Your Search, and Back to the Top (or something similar) would make this HTML page much more cool, in my view.

CUI W3 Catalog

http://cuiwww.unige.ch/w3catalog

The University of Geneva's University Center for Information (well, *Centre Universitaire d'Informatique*) maintains a database of Web sites, with more than 12,000 sites indexed in a format similar to Yahoo. Figure 10-14 shows what you see when you pop into this site.

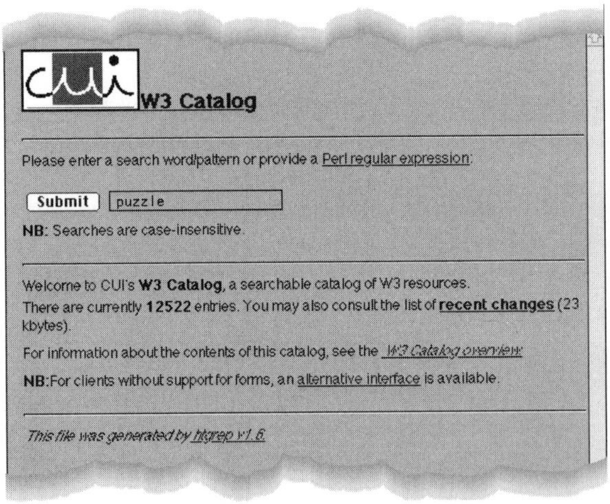

Figure 10-14: CUI W3 home page.

The format is simple, but the result is pleasing. Figure 10-15 shows the result of the *puzzle* search, which leaves a bit to be desired (an indication of how many matches are listed in this file, for example, would be useful).

Figure 10-15: Result of puzzle search in CUI W3.

As it turns out, only three matches for *puzzle* exist in the CUI World Wide Web database, suggesting that it has the least comprehensive Web database of the different search engines that I visited, or perhaps they have something against puzzles for some mysterious reason.

Registering with Web Search Sites

Clearly, the search sites I've discussed here take different approaches to indexing the Web (which means your data). So which site should you register with? All of them. Why not? All the sites are free, and lots of people will use each service to find information, which may just be your own home page.

Joining Yahoo

To join Yahoo, simply connect to the Web page at `http://yahoo.com/yahoo/bin/add`, as shown in Figure 10-16. Fill in all the blanks, and your site will be added after the administrative folks have a glance at your entry.

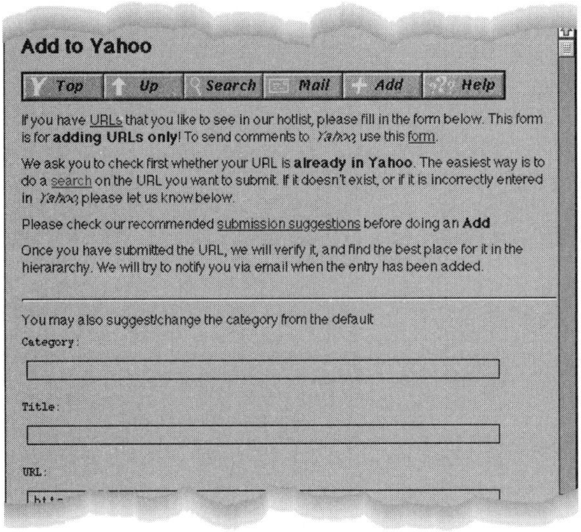

Figure 10-16: Adding your site to Yahoo.

Joining Lycos

To join the Lycos database, you need to connect to `http://lycos.cs.cmu.edu/lycos-register.html`, as shown in Figure 10-17. Then enter the URL for your site, which the system will visit and catalog within a week or so.

Figure 10-17: Adding your site to Lycos.

Joining WebCrawler

WebCrawler allows you to add your site by connecting to `http://webcrawler.cs.washington.edu/WebCrawler/SubmitURLS.html` (see Figure 10-18). As with Lycos, simply enter the URL for your site; the system then visits and indexes your site automatically.

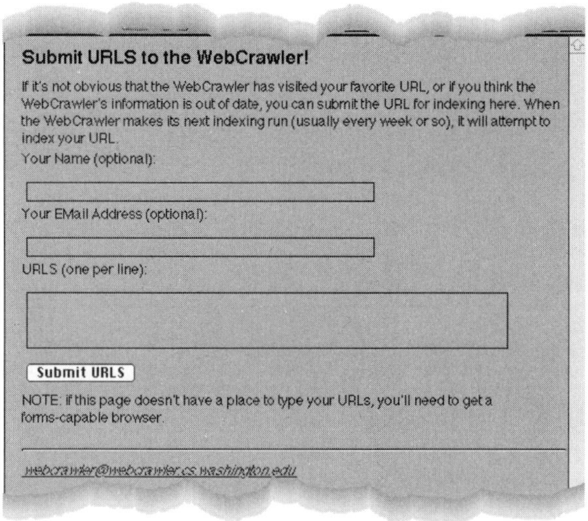

Figure 10-18: Adding your site to the WebCrawler.

Joining EINet Galaxy

EINet Galaxy has its own spot for you to enter your URL information, at `http://www.einet.net/annotate-help.html`. The form looks like Figure 10-19.

Joining CUI W3

Finally, traveling to the Swiss World Wide Web Catalog informs you that the CUI W3 Catalog is built up from the NCSA What's New page, the NCSA Starting Points page, the CERN Virtual Library Subject Catalog, Koster's Aliweb, Yanoff's Internet Services List, and various other spots. Therefore, a listing in the CUI W3 Catalog should be automatic if you're listed at one of these other sites, many of which you will visit in the next chapter.

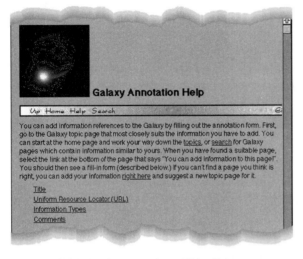

Figure 10-19: *Adding your site to ElNet Galaxy.*

Producing Index-Friendly Web Information

Although much of the work of hooking into the Web's search systems involves filling out some forms and otherwise mailing your URL to specific addresses, you can use some design strategies to create cool and useful Web sites.

First, expect future Web-crawler-type search engines to index purely from the `<TITLE>` portion of your page in a desire to keep the amount of data manageable, so the more meaningful your title is, the more likely that your site will be found when people search for you. To wit, if you're busy creating a site that explores the intricacies of coffee roasting, `<TITLE>Coffee Roasting: The Quest for the Perfect Cup</TITLE>` is better (and more interesting) than `<TITLE>The Coffee Home Page</TITLE>`.

I recommend against using the phrases home page and Web in your page's title at all.

Remember that titles are used not only by some search tools, but they are also what users see as the name of your site when they save your URL to their hotlists. A hotlist full of titles such as The Internet Mall, All About Starbucks, Digital Games Review, and Sony Consumer Electronics offers a great deal more information with less clutter than Ray-o-Vac World Wide Web Page or Stanford University Web Home Page.

Some wit and verve can help, too. Which page would *you* rather visit?

- ❑ Home Page for Pete Nesterenko
- ❑ Who Is This Pete Nesterenko Guy?
- ❑ My Home Page

Needless to say, that last one offers no information about the the Web page and should be avoided like the plague.

Finally, don't forget to have the first paragraph of text in your home page contain a meaningful description of the contents therein; since some of the Web index systems grab the first few sentences, carefully crafting them will help ensure people find your information when they search the various spots listed in this chapter.

• •

This chapter has given you a chance to explore some of the most valuable World Wide Web search tools and learn how to ensure that your new Web information is included in their databases. There are, of course, more Web search engines than I list in this chapter, but the ones here should give you a valuable starting spot for your own searches, and are definitely key spots to register your own Web documents to ensure others can find you! The next chapter continues the discussion by talking about more general-purpose Web starting points and "what's new" pages that can help you spread the word about your site.

Announcing Your Site

This chapter explores avenues for announcing and promoting your Web pages on the Net and for generating visitors and traffic. The Internet contains a huge variety of sites to visit, and that's great until you begin to think about how to get people to visit *your* cool new Web site.

In this chapter

- ❏ Cool "what's new" pages
- ❏ Other cool Web indexes
- ❏ Business-only sites
- ❏ Fee-based advertising spots
- ❏ An important mailing list

This chapter can only scratch the surface, of course. The World Wide Web is growing so quickly that the best I can offer here is a snapshot of what was going on when I wrote this chapter. Still, if you use the sites in this chapter as starting points for your own exploration, you'll be well ahead of the game.

11

Cool What's New Pages

This section gives you the scoop on what I consider to be the best and most important "what's new" pages on the Web.

The Mosaic/GNN What's New Page

http://www.ncsa.uiuc.edu/SDG/Software/Mosaic/Docs/whats-new.html

If there is a single, definitive spot for announcing your presence on the World Wide Web, it's the NCSA Mosaic What's New Page. The National Center for Supercomputing Applications at the University of Illinois at Urbana-Champaign is *the* happening spot for announcements on the Web (see Figure 11-1).

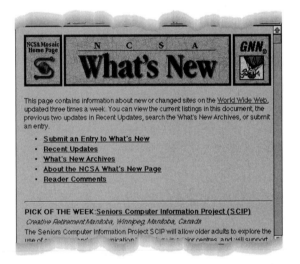

Figure 11-1: What's new at NCSA.

What you don't see in Figure 11-1 is just how massive this page of information is. When I checked it at the end of April 1995, I found that it contained more than 140 entries, just on that one page. The entries are sorted alphabetically, and that's not necessarily the best strategy in my book — I seek information by topic, not by company, organization, or Web pages per se. The NCSA Mosaic What's New Page is an important spot for your announcement, but don't be surprised if very few people actually *see* your announcement in the jumble.

> You can improve your chances of being seen simply by having a Web page name that starts with a letter early in the alphabet. Aardvarks Online, for example, is going to be seen by more browsers than Xylophone Factory.

Keeping track of what's new on the Web is *more* than a full-time job, and the NCSA team didn't want to lose their focus on application development. So, NCSA transferred responsibility for running the what's-new information to O'Reilly and Associates, which maintains the GNN site, the way cool Global Network Navigator. GNN is a Web-based online magazine that's well worth checking out for its great Web design. The site is at `http://gnn.com/gnn/GNNhome.html`, and the current first page is shown in Figure 11-2.

Figure 11-2: Global Network Navigator.

Special Internet Connections

http://www.uwm.edu/Mirror/inet.services.html

Scott Yanoff, while a student at the University of Wisconsin in Madison, started a terrific list called Special Internet Connections. Now a Web Developer for SpectraCom, Scott continues to maintain his great list of useful, valuable spots on the Internet. As part of his work, Yanoff has made available a fascinating Web spot that offers a directory of some of the coolest spots on the Web. (He was also kind enough to write the Foreword to this book.)

Figure 11-3 shows the utilitarian design of Yanoff's Special Internet Connections Web document, including a tantalizing glimpse of the many categorizations that his list features.

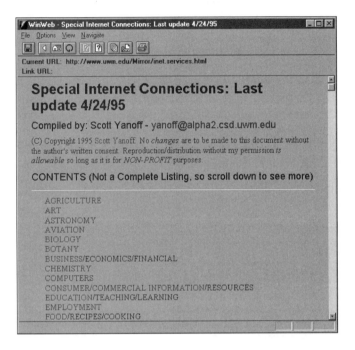

Figure 11-3: Scott Yanoff's Special Internet Connections.

If you have created a site that is of public interest, Scott Yanoff will be delighted to hear from you and will consider adding you to his database of sites. If you're creating a commercial site, though, he's most likely to forward your announcement to the Internet Mall database (discussed later in this chapter).

The Netscape What's New Page

http://home.mcom.com/home/whats-new.html

After your introduction in Chapter 9 to the cool new HTML features found in the Netscape Navigator, you shouldn't be surprised that Netscape is one of the most popular browsers. When you first run it, the Navigator takes you to a page in the Netscape site (by default). Among the many cool Web pages on Netscape's system is the What's New page.

Unfortunately, it didn't take more than about six months for the Netscape Communications people to realize that keeping track of what's new is a huge job, so they cut a deal with the two chaps at Stanford University who run Yahoo to work in parallel on the process. Then a few months later, when Yahoo spun off as a company, Netscape returned to their original strategy of having its own What's New page, only now it only lists sites that are new and demonstrate advanced uses of HTML. As you see in Figure 11-4, the Netscape What's New page is surprisingly low-key, but does include a prominent sponsor advert.

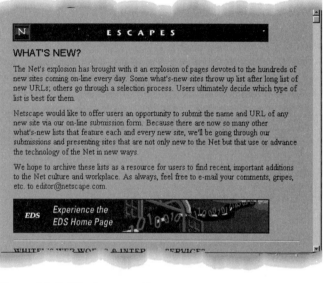

Figure 11-4: What's new at Netscape.

Frankly, odds are Netscape isn't likely to accept your announcement of what you've done on the Web, but I still recommend it as a good place to start your own exploration.

Other Cool Web Indexes

Beyond lists of new sites, some spots on the Web are devoted to indexing Web sites by category. Here are some of the best ones.

World Wide Web Virtual Library

http://www.w3.org/hypertext/DataSources/bySubject/Overview.html

The Swiss group that created the World Wide Web and the original version of HTML also designed an attractive, helpful reference site that organizes Web information by category. The site is called the Virtual Library. Figure 11-5 shows the top of the Virtual Library home page.

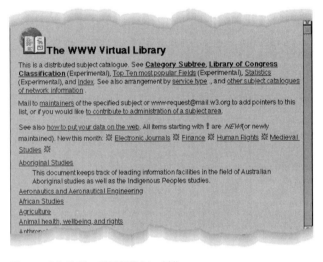

Figure 11-5: The WWW Virtual Library.

Rather than try to maintain all the information themselves, W3 opted — wisely, in my view — to break the material into categories and have different people maintain the subject catalogs. To have *your* Web site added to the Virtual Library, therefore, you must track down the person who maintains the appropriate part.

Suppose that you're interested in information about tarot readings, having just created a cool Web site dedicated to the subject. Scroll down the first page of the Virtual Library, and you'll find a section called Fortune Telling, with Tarot appearing as an option. Click on Tarot, and you're transported to the Tarot information area at UCLA (of all places). You can quickly find that the person who runs this site is Jonathan Katz, as shown at the bottom of Figure 11-6. Send an e-mail message to Katz, and your new Tarot Web site could very well be listed as another information source for Web users.

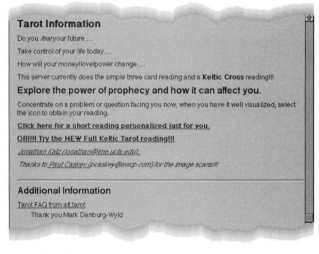

Figure 11-6: Tarot information from UCLA.

The Living City

http://www.cadvision.com/top.html

An English company called CADVision maintains a very nice, totally different type of Web hot-spot index called The Living City. Figure 11-7 shows the opening graphic (which, by the way, is a great example of the weird and funky things you can do within the Web environment).

Figure 11-7: The Living City.

Getting around within The Living City is easy. I recommend that the Internet Hierarchy be your first stop; it provides yet another hierarchical index to the thousands of sites on the Web and beyond. Figuring out how to get your Web page listed at The Living City, however, is somewhat difficult. The best strategy seems to be sending an e-mail message to `city@cadvision.com`, indicating the name of your site, its URL, and any other information that you want to have included. Alternatively, try connecting directly to their new link form at `http://daffy.cadvision.com/newlinks.html`

Global Online Directory

http://www.cityscape.co.uk/gold/indexdir.html

CityScape Internet Services of London, England, is trying to create a central spot where people can search for information on the Internet by hosting a yellow pages-like database of classified advertisements. Unlike other Web sites, CityScape attempts to keep its listings current by purging all links after a specified period (usually 90 days). Figure 11-8 shows the entry point for this interesting spot.

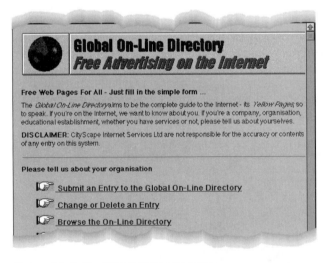

Figure 11-8: The Global Online Directory.

For my taste, access to the CityScape site is a little slow, from the U.S. anyway. The graphics sometimes don't load properly, due to what appears to be transmission errors.

Miscellaneous Index Spots

In this section, I list some of the more unusual Web indexes.

City.Net

http://www.city.net/

This site in Portland, Oregon, has another spin on things: It seeks to organize information by locale. The idea is neat, and the graphics are quite attractive, as shown in Figure 11-9. Still, a nagging voice in my head keeps asking why the geographic location of a Web site should be relevant in cyberspace.

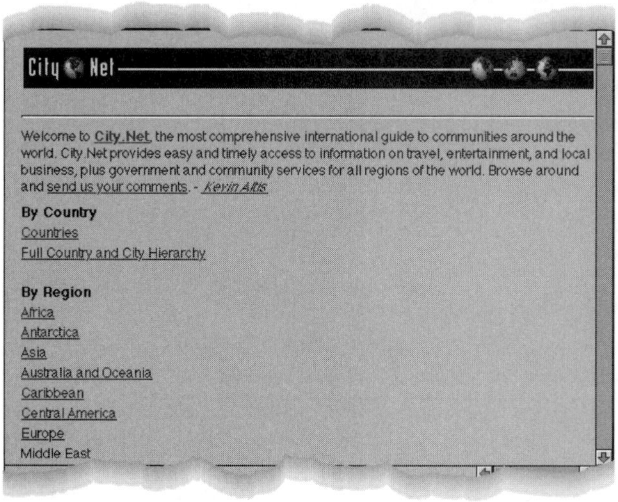

Figure 11-9: City.Net.

If the information at your new site is geographical in nature — a photo tour of a local national park, a list of favorite cafes in your city, or what have you — City.Net may be a great place to add your information.

Inter-Links

http://alpha.acast.nova.edu/start.html

To demonstrate that you don't need to be a computer expert to maintain a cool and valuable Web site, Inter-Links was created and is run by Rob Kabacoff, Ph.D., of the Center for Psychological Studies at Nova Southeastern University in Fort Lauderdale, Florida. Figure 11-10 demonstrates that Inter-Links is a straightforward index to information sites on the Web.

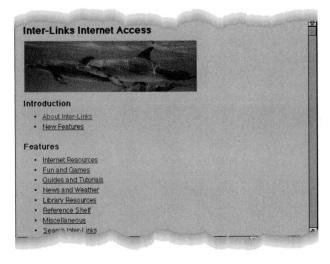

Figure 11-10: Navigate the Web with Inter-Links.

Figure 11-10 also illustrates something else: A Web site can offer a great deal of useful information without being particularly cool. (I expect that, by now, you could write a page like this with your eyes closed.)

Web of Wonder

http://www.digimark.net/wow

Another spin on a hierarchical index is the Web of Wonder, maintained by Lance Weitzel with assistance from Digital Marketing Corporation. Figure 11-11 reveals that the site offers another unordered bullet list of topics, each topic listing the sites that Weitzel has visited.

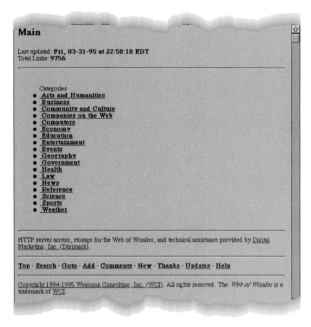

Figure 11-11: Web of Wonder.

The InterNIC Directory of Directories

http://ds.internic.net/ds/dsdirofdirs.html

The Internet may appear to be an amazing anarchy, but there *is* a place with some semblance of order, a slight method to the madness. What little control exists originates at the Internet Network Information Center, known informally as the InterNIC. InterNIC subcontracts with different vendors. The directory information is run by AT&T, as Figure 11-12 makes obvious.

This site has a ton of great stuff, but AT&T dropped the ball in the grand scheme, because the directory, believe it or not, doesn't have any actual links to other sites! If you find a directory that sounds interesting, you have to either print out that page or write down the URL that you want, just to type it again in your browser — not a very cool arrangement, in my opinion. Still, this site is an important one, and you'll want to include your information here if that information is relevant.

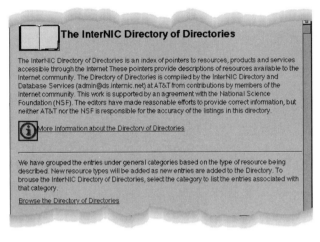

Figure 11-12: The InterNIC Directory of Directories.

Business-Only Sites

This section contains sites that are dedicated to commerce.

The Internet Mall

http://www.mecklerweb.com/imall/

A site that's near and dear to my heart is the Internet Mall, the only commercial directory on the Internet that focuses exclusively on companies that actually sell products or services. It's also a favorite of mine because, in fact, I run the Internet Mall! If you have a business venture that's just joined the Web, you definitely should let me know so I can add you to the Internet Mall. Figure 11-13 shows the opening screen.

The design of this site shows one way that you can work with small graphics and still have an interesting layout: make your button graphics meaningful.

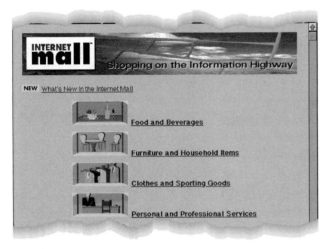

Figure 11-13: The Internet Mall.

Open Market's Commercial Site Index

http://www.directory.net/

If your business is on the Web, and you want to ensure that you're in the electronic equivalent of the yellow pages, the Open Market Commercial Site Index is the best choice available (see Figure 11-14). Listing almost 1,500 commercial sites, the Open Market site is a great place to start if you're looking for other companies on the Web.

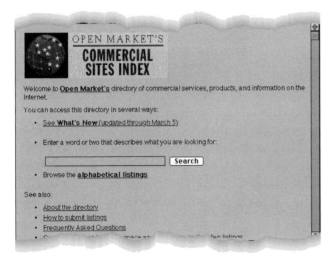

Figure 11-14: Open Market's Commercial Site Index.

The design of the Open Market site is rather unusual; it's the only important announcement site that has a search input box near the top of the layout. I don't particularly like the design, because I like to browse by category. But when things are organized purely by the name of the business, this approach is better than just having a long list of names.

Apollo Advertising

http://apollo.co.uk/

A very different approach — one reminiscent of City.Net, shown earlier in this chapter — is the Apollo Advertisement site, located in England (see Figure 11-15). Notice particularly the size of the world graphic and the very attractive APOLLO graphic at the top of the page. The prose at this site (including frequent typographical errors) is frustrating, but Apollo Advertising still can be a terrific spot to advertise your new Web site.

Figure 11-15: Apollo Advertising.

If you scroll below the map of the world, you see a list of bullet items for each country. That list is invaluable for people with slower connections who opt not to preload all graphics before working with a Web page.

Don't forget that some users may not load the graphics. Always make sure your design tries to take that fact into account.

BizWeb

http://www.bizweb.com/

BizWeb offers an index on the very first page of the Web site (see Figure 11-16).

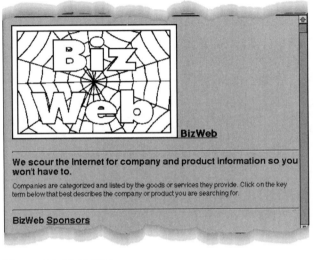

Figure 11-16: BizWeb.

You can see that the designer got a *little* carried away with the opening graphic. Rather than functioning as a cool design element, the graphic forces users to scroll down the page to find any interesting information — not the best design, in my view. The organization of shops and companies at this site, however, is very good, and BizWeb is a good spot to list your commercial Web site.

Product.Com

http://www.product.com/

Taking a slightly different approach, Product.Com offers a central spot for product-related information. The majority of stuff at Product.Com is computer-related (probably no big surprise, given the current demographics of the Internet), but you may find some surprises if you dig around a little. Figure 11-17 offers a snapshot of this site.

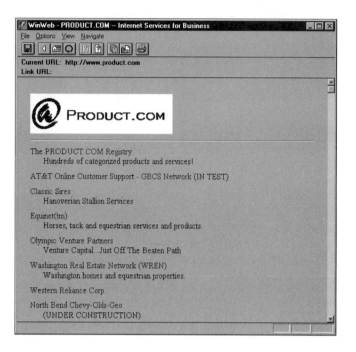

Figure 11-17: Product.Com product information.

The design of the Product.Com page is pretty cool (I really like the logo), but I wish that the design somehow highlighted the search and registration options, which I feel are lost in the bullet list that dominates the page.

Fee-Based Advertising Spots

Plenty of Web sites charge you money for a listing and/or require you to join their organization in order to get a link from their page to yours. Are these spots worth it? You'll have to decide for yourself. If you're a small entrepreneur, you probably won't be able to ante up the fees.

Many fee-based sites do, however, offer interesting approaches to Web page design. An example is MecklerWeb, from MecklerMedia (see Figure 11-18). A listing at this site, like any of the commercial spots, isn't cheap. But if you have a compelling need to generate traffic on your Web site, joining one of these sites can be the way to go.

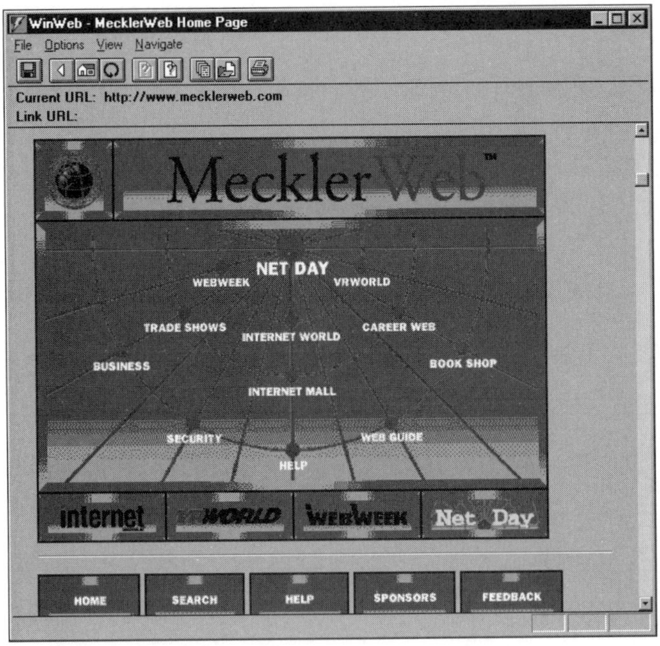

Figure 11-18: MecklerWeb.

To visit MecklerWeb yourself, go to http://www.mecklerweb.com/.

An Important Mailing List

Although most of the places to announce your Web site are, naturally, on the World Wide Web, there is one mailing list to which you should not only send your announcement, but should also read. That list is the invaluable Net-Happenings mailing list, run by the InterNIC (Internet Network Information Center).

You can subscribe to Net-Happenings by sending e-mail to majordomo@is.internic.net with **subscribe net-happenings** in the body of the message. To submit your new-site announcement, send a note directly to net-happenings@is.internic.net. Here's a typical announcement, about a law library that's accessible via the Web:

```
Date: Wed, 19 Apr 95 11:43:00 -0600
From: Fred Barnhart <fbarnhar@kentlaw.edu>
Subject: ChicagoKent College of Law Library

The ChicagoKent College of Law Library is pleased to announce
public access to its homepage at...

             http://www.kentlaw.edu/lir

By linking to the site, attorneys, law students, graduate
students and librarians can access information about:

            - the Legal Information Center
            - the Library of International Relations
            - LOIS (the library's imaging system)
            - Reference and Research services
            - ExMentis (copyright tracking software)
            - Subscriber services
            - Document Delivery
            - Chicago's Consulates and the countries they represent

Check out our site!
```

Depending on your Internet habits and tastes, a better strategy may be to check out the Net-Happenings Usenet newsgroup using your favorite newsreader program. On Usenet, the group is called `comp.internet.net-happenings`.

The Best Way

The best way to publicize your new Web site is to become active in the Internet community, and to be sure to include your site in all your documents, advertisements, and in any other materials you use to interact with your peers, friends, and customers. Find the cool Web sites in your area of interest and ask them to include pointers to your information. Almost all sites will do that for free, particularly if you agree to list them at your site, too.

The next chapter gives you a taste of some of the more advanced (and complicated) capabilities of HTML and the Web, including an introduction to forms and database queries, a list of items that will change when HTML 3 is released, and Netscape custom information. The chapter also covers URL pointers to online documents that define up-to-the-minute specifications and applications.

Where to Next?

This chapter provides an introduction to forms and database queries and includes a list of items that will be changing with HTML 3.0 when it is released. I also discuss URL pointers to online documents that define up-to-the-minute specifications and applications.

In this chapter

- ❑ An introduction to image maps
- ❑ An introduction to HTML forms
- ❑ The common gateway interface inside your Web server
- ❑ HTML+ extensions
- ❑ More future directions

There are some complex Web tricks that I only discuss topically: image maps and forms processing. Why? I believe that the tools for creating and processing those HTML elements are improving so quickly that anything I talk about here will be obsolete by the time you pick up this book. Further, the methods of processing image maps and forms vary so dramatically among platforms that it would take quite an explanation to cover even the basics of the top three Web server systems. I don't want to just skip the material, however, and you should at least see how various programs allow you to extend the hypertext metaphor.

An Introduction to Image Maps

In the last two chapters, you learned about several sites on the Web that eschew mundane bulleted lists in favor of sexy, all-encompassing graphics. When you click a particular spot on the graphic, the server somehow knows where you clicked and moves you to the appropriate spot on the server.

This impressive trick is performed through the use of an ISMAP extension to the IMG specification and a companion MAP file, which specifies all the known regions in the picture and associates them with specific URLs. ISMAP indicates that the image you're including is a 'mapped' image; clicking on different spots on the image produce different results.

A very simple example consists of three parts: the graphic, a few lines of HTML to specify the image map, and the MAP document. For example, a map of Arizona could enable users to choose between Phoenix and Tucson as a travel destination by clicking on the appropriate city on the map.

Following is the HTML. Notice the ISMAP addition to the arizona.gif image instruction.

```
<CENTER>
<IMG SRC="arizona-head.gif"><BR>
<A HREF="http://mysite.com/arizona.map">
<IMG ISMAP SRC="arizona.gif"></A><BR>
Where would you like to go on vacation?
</CENTER>
```

When displayed, the preceding snippet produces the graphic shown in Figure 12-1. Notice that the map is displayed as a typical GIF image, without any special border or other indication that it is, in fact, an image map or anything other than a regular included graphic. Having an entire image as a single button, however, results in the standard colored border.

Figure 12-1: A clickable image map.

The next step in creating our Arizona travel overview map is to identify the spots on the graphic that are the center of the desired hot spots or specific points on the image that are to have specific actions. I loaded the map into a simple graphics editor and, by moving the mouse pointer to the city spots for Tucson and Phoenix, I ascertained that they are x,y coordinates 158,208 (Tucson) and 123,160 (Phoenix). (The coordinate 0,0 is the upper left-hand corner of the image.)

Next, I decide which geometric figure I want to use to define the limits of the hot spot. I'll opt for the circles shown in Table 12-1 since they allow me to easily define a region around each of the two cities identified. Other choices could have been squares, rectangles, or others, as shown.

Table 12-1	Shapes Available for ISMAP Files
Name	**Coordinates Needed in .MAP File on Server**
Circle	Center-point radius or, for NCSA image maps, center, edge point
Poly	List of vertices, maximum 100
Rect	Upper-left lower-right
Point	x,y

Here's where things get a bit more puzzling. The specific format of the .MAP file, the file that defines all the active points on the image, is dependent on the kind of Web server that's running on the server machine. Up to this point, you've learned about HTML tags that work differently with different browsers, but this is the first example (in this book) of one that varies by the program at the other end, the server.

There are two main choices of Web server: CERN or NCSA. CERN, as you'll recall, is the Swiss organization that invented the World Wide Web, and NCSA is the group that developed the popular Mosaic Web browser. Because I happen to be using a CERN-style Web server to present the Arizona Travel information Web pages, I have to use the CERN format definitions.

CERN servers use the first method of specifying the circle in the table. I need to indicate the center point and radius for each circular hot-spot I want. CERN-style .MAP files also use the general layout method/coordinates/URL, with points surrounded by parenthesis. All of this is shown in the actual `image.map` file shown below:

```
default countryside.html
circle (123,160) 20 phoenix.html
circle (158,208) 20 tucson.html
```

The two circles defined will let users click near the cities of Phoenix or Tucson and learn more about those specific places. That's the second and third line above. The Phoenix entry is exemplary: the region defined for this action within the graphic image (`arizona.gif`) is a circle centered at 123,160, it has a 20-pixel radius, and any clicks within it result in the user being transferred to the URL `phoenix.html`. Since users might well click outside of the two spots I've defined, I also added a default action with the 'default' specification; users that click on any area that is not covered by the two circles will be connected to the `countryside.html` page.

By contrast, if I were using an NCSA server, my map file would look somewhat different, because NCSA changes the order of fields to method/URL/coordinates and omits the parentheses around map points. Consider the changes to the specification for the circular hotspots:

```
default http://mysite.com/countryside.html
circle phoenix.html 123,160 123,180
circle tucson.html 158,208 158,228
```

The circle method in this example also requires a change. Instead of the logical center+radius approach that is used with the CERN MAP format, NCSA wants two points identified: one at the center of the circle, and the other somewhere along its edge. That's why these change. Personally, I prefer the CERN format for MAP files since it's a lot easier to identify the center of a circle and then indicate how big it should be.

Although defining and calculating all the points in complex ISMAP graphics may be tedious, the result can be tremendously effective, as you saw in the attractive opening graphics of many of the sites featured in Chapter 11. I'm partial to the opening map of the MecklerWeb site (see Figure 12-2).

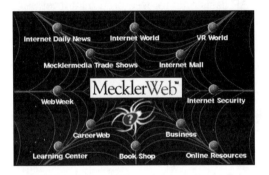

Figure 12-2: MecklerWeb opening map image.

The NCSA-server format ISMAP data underlying that file is complex. If you take a deep breath and look at the data line by line, however, the following example makes a lot of sense:

```
default http://www.mecklerweb.com/home.htm
rect http://www.mecklerweb.com/mags/iw/news/newsmenu.htm 12,13 148,57
rect http://www.mecklerweb.com/mags/iw/iwhome.htm 168,13 278,58
rect http://www.mecklerweb.com/vr.htm 322,8 407,59
rect http://www.mecklerweb.com/imall/imall.htm 259,61 358,106
rect http://www.mecklerweb.com/shows/showhome.htm 42,60 235,106
rect http://www.mecklerweb.com/mweb/mweb.htm 136,113 315,159
rect http://www.mecklerweb.com/security/security.htm 317,126 429,173
rect http://www.mecklerweb.com/mags/ww/wwhome.htm 38,123 121,174
rect http://www.mecklerweb.com/mags/iw/learning/learning.htm 24,227
140,270
```

```
rect http://www.mecklerweb.com/books/bookshom.htm 187,228 265,270
rect http://www.mecklerweb.com/mags/iw/resource/resource.htm 305,229
437,270
rect http://www.mecklerweb.com/biz/bizhome.htm 269,186 345,227
rect http://www.mecklerweb.com/about/help.htm 169,160 256,210
poly http://www.mecklerweb.com/careerwb/careerwb.htm 100,188 100,225
182,225 179,216 169,207 155,183 100,188
```

Seeing the complexity of the preceding map file, you can understand why specific tools that help you create ISMAP data files are wonderful things and very time-saving. Even better, you can obtain a variety of different ISMAP assistants for free on the Internet, whether you're on a Macintosh, a UNIX workstation, or a PC running Windows. The best place to start your exploration is on Yahoo at the following address:

```
http://www.yahoo.com/Computers/World_Wide_Web/Programming/Imagemaps
```

An Introduction to HTML Forms

Image maps, as shown above, are one of the HTML extensions that allow for more interactive Web design. The other popular extension is support for forms, Web pages that let users actually enter information and send it back to the server site. The forms in question can range from a single text box for entering e-mail to the person who runs the server to a complex multipart worksheet that offers powerful search or submission capabilities.

Two basic types of forms exist in HTML — GET and POST forms — and they revolve around the way that the information is presented to the Common Gateway Interface (CGI) script back at the server. I'll explain the difference in the following section. For now, look at the design and specification of forms themselves. The Common Gateway Interface is the part of the Web server that actually receives and processes the information sent in an HTML form.

HTML forms are surrounded by the `<FORM ACTION=url METHOD=method>` and `</FORM>` tags. The *url* points to the remote file or application used for digesting the information, and *method* is either GET or POST. In a nutshell, GET only works for small amounts of data since the information in the form is tucked into a URL that's returned to the Web server. By contrast, a POST form sends the information back as an actual data stream, allowing for considerably more feedback from the user.

Inside the <FORM> your Web page can contain any standard HTML formatting information and a bunch of new tags specific to forms. The various new tags let you define the many different elements of your form, as shown in Table 12-2.

Table 12-2	FORM Tags and Options in HTML
Tag	**Meaning**
<INPUT>	Text or other data-input field
TYPE =	type of INPUT entry field
NAME =	symbolic name of field value
VALUE =	default content of text field
CHECKED =	button/box checked by default
SIZE =	number of characters in text field
MAXLENGTH =	maximum characters accepted
<SELECT>	Grouped checkboxes
<TEXTAREA>	Multiline text-entry field

The variety of different options within the <INPUT> tag can be confusing, but the way to understand the overloaded <INPUT> tag is to realize that although the entire form system was supposed to be included within <INPUT> specifiers, SELECT and TEXTAREA just didn't fit in.

Current Web browsers support six <INPUT> types, each of which produces a different type of output. The four user input types are:

❏ TEXT is the default, with SIZE used to specify the default size of the box that is created.

❏ PASSWORD is a text field with the user input displayed as asterisks or bullets for security. MAXLENGTH can be used to specify the maximum number of characters entered in the password.

❏ CHECKBOX offers a single (ungrouped) checkbox; CHECKED enables you to specify whether or not the box should be checked by default. VALUE specifies the text associated with the checkbox.

❏ RADIO displays a toggle button; different radio buttons with the same NAME= value are grouped automatically, so that only one button in the group can be selected.

The two most important <INPUT> types are:

❑ SUBMIT, which produces a push button in the form that, when clicked, submits the entire form content to the remote server.

❑ RESET, which enables users to clear the contents of all fields in the form.

<SELECT> is most like an unordered list, with a </SELECT> partner and <OPTION> denoting each of the items therein. You must specify a NAME that uniquely identifies the overall selection within the <SELECT> tag itself. Optionally, you can specify SIZE, indicating how many items should be displayed at once (if there are more than can be displayed the list becomes a pop-up menu instead), and MULTIPLE, indicating that it's OK for users to select more than one option. If a default value exists, add SELECTED to the <OPTION> tag (as in <OPTION SELECTED>) to indicate that value.

The <TEXTAREA> tag also has several options, starting with the mandatory NAME tag that denotes the symbolic name of the field. You also can specify ROWS and COLS to indicate the size of the resulting text field, with units in characters. This tag also is a paired tag, partnered by </TEXTAREA>. Any text between the two tags is displayed as the default information in the text box.

Forms can be quite complex to fine-tune and get right. Consider the following HTML text and the way it's displayed. This form could be used as the beginning of a Web order-counter form for Dave's Virtual Online Deli:

```
<FORM ACTION="process-form.cgi" METHOD=POST>
<B>Dave's Virtual Deli — The Order Menu</B>
<HR>
Your name? <INPUT TYPE=text NAME="name" SIZE=30>
<BR>
Secret code: <INPUT TYPE=password NAME="password">
<HR>
<B>What kind of sandwich? </B>
<SELECT NAME="Sandwich">
<OPTION>(none)
<OPTION>Turkey on a croissant
<OPTION>Ham and cheese on wheat
<OPTION>Veggie on nine-grain
</SELECT>
<BR>
<B>Any soup? </B>
<SELECT NAME="Soup">
<OPTION>(none)
```

```
<OPTION>Tomato and rice
<OPTION>Cream of asparagus
<OPTION>Lentil Madness
</SELECT>
<P>
How you'll pay:
<INPUT TYPE=radio NAME="payment" VALUE="visa">Visa
<INPUT TYPE=radio NAME="payment" VALUE="mastercard">MasterCard
<INPUT TYPE=radio NAME="payment" VALUE="account" CHECKED>Account
<INPUT TYPE=radio NAME="payment" VALUE="dishes">Wash dishes
<HR>
<INPUT TYPE=checkbox NAME="firstorder" VALUE="firstorder">
First time ordering from the Virtual Deli?<BR>
<INPUT TYPE=submit NAME="submit" VALUE="Let's eat">
<INPUT TYPE=reset NAME="reset" VALUE="clear">
</FORM>
```

Figure 12-3 shows the preceding form with some of the information filled out by a hungry user. The secret code value would be displayed in bullets, even though the user entered an actual password, and the pop-up menu for sandwich and soup types is automatically included by the browser itself. The user could opt to pay by washing dishes, having seen that the default option was to put the bill on his account (as specified by the CHECKED option in the HTML).

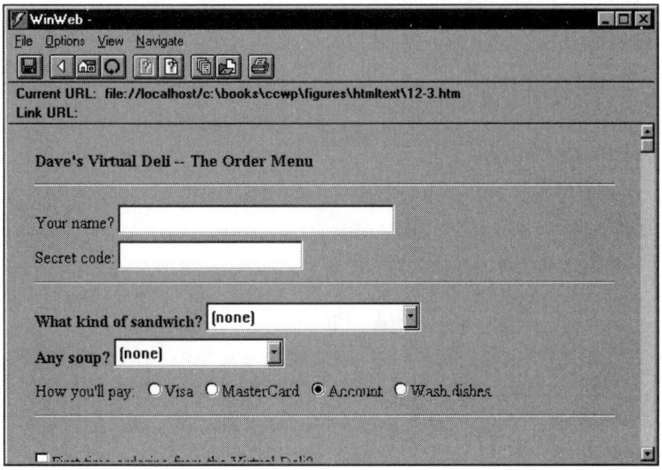

Figure 12-3: The Virtual Deli order form.

Except for the `<TEXTAREA>` option, the following example demonstrates most of the facets of an HTML form. It's an example of a common way to enable users to send e-mail to the Web designer or maintainer:

```
<FORM ACTION="e-mail-form.cgi" METHOD=POST>
<H2>Send Feedback to the Designer!</H2>
Enter your comments below, and click send it when you finish.
<HR>
<TEXTAREA NAME="feedback" ROWS=5 COLS=70>
This is a vastly cool Web site!
</TEXTAREA>
<HR>
<INPUT TYPE=submit NAME="submit" VALUE="send it">
<INPUT TYPE=reset NAME="reset" VALUE="clear">
</FORM>
```

When accessed by a browser, the preceding HTML appears as shown in Figure 12-4. You can see that the default text shows up in the input box. (My guess is that if I left this text in a form, I'd get a lot of e-mail that simply contained that message.)

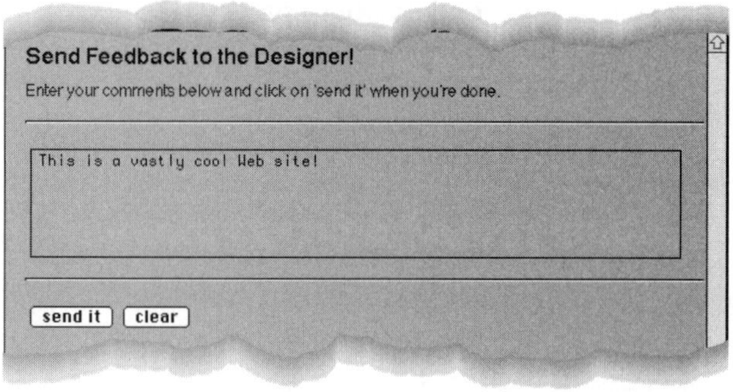

Figure 12-4: An e-mail message-input form.

Before I leave the fun and interesting area of forms entry, I'll provide one more example. If you want to have a single entry box for search capability, you can use the HTML shortcut `<ISINDEX>`, which produces a single input box at the top, prefaced by the default text `This is a searchable index. Enter search keywords:` and surrounded by horizontal rules, as follows:

```
You've found the Oxford English Dictionary online!
<ISINDEX>
You can browse this or look up a term directly.
```

This HTML snippet produces the screen shown in Figure 12-5. This isn't necessarily preferable to the more complex form items, because you have little control of layout, submission form name, and similar items. In some applications, however, the ease of generation can be quite valuable.

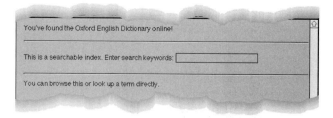

Figure 12-5: <ISINDEX> adds an instant input box.

Just as valuable, <ISINDEX> is an example of a single text-input field that allows most browsers to map the Return or Enter key to the SUBMIT option. Instead of having to click the submit button (which, remember, can have any text you'd like by specifying that in the <INPUT TYPE=submit VALUE=your text> tag), typing the information and pressing Return or Enter submits the information from the form to the remote Web server. The search option in Yahoo exhibits this behavior, too, although it doesn't use the <ISINDEX> feature.

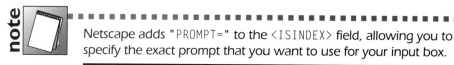

Netscape adds "PROMPT=" to the <ISINDEX> field, allowing you to specify the exact prompt that you want to use for your input box.

The Common Gateway Interface Inside Your Web Server

You've now seen that you can have fun creating forms as part of a cool Web site. When the time comes to consider how to process the information that users are submitting, however, you get into some sticky, system-dependent questions.

With image maps, you saw that the format of the map file depends on the type of server that you're running. CERN and NCSA servers have different expectations for the information in the map file.

The interface behind forms is even more complex, because the very environment that you work with when processing the form depends heavily on the operating system used on the server. Scripting a gateway (hence the *common gateway interface*, or *CGI*, moniker for these scripts) is dramatically different on a UNIX system than it is on a Windows machine or a Macintosh — not to mention Windows NT, Amiga, and other types of servers.

The biggest difference involves what programming languages and tools are available. On a UNIX system, it's quite simple to create a shell script, Perl script, or even a C program or two to process and act on input. Shell scripts aren't even a possibility on a Mac, however, so AppleScript is used instead. Windows machines rely on either a DOS command template or what's known informally as a jacket script. Fortunately, the Perl-interpreted programming language is also available on DOS machines, and that's what I recommend that you use.

As I said earlier, the FORM method has two options: GET and POST. Now I can explain the difference between these options. When a GET method is used, the information is appended to the URL and handed, as such, to the script. All information shows up encoded, following a question mark that's appended to the original URL. POST causes the information to be sent to the server as the content of a data body rather than a long URL. This method is much less common but better when significant amounts of information are to be transmitted. Expect most forms in the future to migrate to use the POST method.

To keep the scope of this explanation reasonable, I'll stick with the GET method to illustrate how the forms shown earlier would be sent to the CGI server script. First, the deli order would be built and submitted as follows:

```
process-form.cgi?name=Umberto%20Eco;pass=mycode;
Sandwich=4;Soup=2;payment=dishes;firstorder
```

The %20 encodes spaces to keep the URL legal. (Remember, spaces aren't allowed in any URL.) Also, you can see that the password was shielded from prying eyes when the user entered the information, but when this information is sent to the server, it's sent as clear text. It would be up to the server script to unravel this tangle of information and process it.

The output of any CGI script is more HTML than is displayed on the user's screen after the user has submitted the form and it's processed by the server. A rough template of a script, therefore, might be like the following example:

```
replace all %20 with ' '
replace all ';' with a return


send request to kitchen
return the following to the user:
<HTML>
<TITLE>It's Cookin'!</TITLE>
Thank you for your order. We're now busy preparing
the meal that you selected. We invite
you to stop by the <B>Virtual Deli</B> in about
15 minutes to pick up your food.
<P>
<I>Thanks again for your support!</I>
<HR>
<A HREF="deli.html">Back to the Deli</A>
</HTML>
```

Of course, processing the information is more complex. Following is a Perl CGI script that processes the simple e-mail submissions from a three-part form: user name ("name"), user e-mail address ("e-mail"), and user comment ("comment"). A script of this form could be used on a UNIX system or on a PC with the Perl language installed.

```
#!/usr/local/bin/perl
$mailer = '/usr/lib/sendmail';  # mailer program
$recipient = 'webmaster';                # who gets feedback mail?
# Print the first part of the return document
print "<HTML>";
print "<TITLE>Thank You for Your Comments!</TITLE>";
print "We try our best to keep this Web server not just up-to-date";
print "but also cool and fun; your comments are invaluable in that";
print "regard, and we are most grateful for your input!";
# get user information from standard input (the server)
read(STDIN, $buffer, $ENV{'CONTENT_LENGTH'});
# Split the name-value pairs into a dynamically allocated array
@info = split(/&/, $buffer);
foreach $pair (@info)
```

```
{
  ($name, $value) = split(/=/, $pair);
  # extract the % encoded info and '+' -> ' ' mapping
  $value =~ tr/+/ /;
  $value =~ s/%([a-fA-F0-9][a-fA-F0-9])/pack("C", hex($1))/eg;
  # save it in DATA array information
  $DATA{$name} = $value;
}
open (MAIL, "|$mailer $recipient") || die "Can't start $mailer!\n";
print MAIL "Subject: Web user comments...\n\n";
print MAIL "Reply-to: $DATA{'e-mail'} ($DATA{'name'})\n";
print MAIL "$DATA{'e-mail'} ($DATA{'name'}) sent:\n";
print MAIL "$DATA{'comments'}";
close (MAIL);
print "<HR><A HREF=\"home.html\">let's go home</A>"
print "</HTML>"
```

A script that produces a similar mailing of user feedback on a Macintosh would most likely be written as an AppleScript script. Rather than having many functions appear in the script, most of the commands in the script rely on AppleScript extensions called OSAX utilities. You need to have quite a few of these extensions to get things to work correctly in most of the scripts that I've seen. Following is the top portion of a very simple AppleScript CGI form processor:

```
on "event WWW_sdoc" given "class post":post_args

  — convert '+' to ' '
  set varList to tokenize post_args with delimiters "+"
  set space_args to item 1 of varList
  set varList to rest of varList
  repeat with x in varList
      set space_args to space_args & " " & x
  end repeat
  set varList to tokenize space_args with delimiters "&"

  — individual items are always name=value. Extract
  repeat with x in varList
      set token to tokenize x with delimiters "=" & ""
      set itemOne to (Decode URL item 1 of token)

      try
```

```
            if (itemOne) is "e-mail" then
                    set e-mail to (Decode URL item 2 of token)
            else if (itemOne) is "name" then
                    set username to (Decode URL item 2 of token)
            else if (itemOne) is "message" then
                    set message to (Decode URL item 2 of token)
            end if
        end try

    end repeat

    send_message("user", "host.com", user, address, message)

    set feedback to "</HTML><HEAD><TITLE>Thank you!</TITLE></HEAD>"
    set feedback to feedback &
    "<BODY><H2>Thanks for your message!</H2>"
    set feedback to feedback & username &
    ", your mail has been delivered. "
    set feedback to feedback & "</BODY></HTML>"
    return feedback

end "event WWW_sdoc"
```

Hop over to http://www.yahoo.com/Computers/World_Wide_Web/ Programming to see all the different options for CGI processing tools, organized by platform. Quite a few helper programs are available.

HTML+ Extensions

One final topic I'd like to touch on before wrapping up this book is the exciting extensions to HTML that are coming down the pike — first as HTML+, and then as HTML 3 add-ons. HTML+ extensions should be familiar to you — almost all of them are already included in Netscape and are demonstrated in Chapter 9. HTML 3 adds tables, background colors, and more capabilities, and is slated for support and release about the time this book is published in the summer of 1995.

Overall, the additions showing up in HTML+ seem to be aimed at specific niches, rather than major new functions. Table 12-3 offers an overview.

Table 12-3	**HTML+ Extensions and Additions**	
Tag	**Partner Tag**	**Meaning**
<ABBREV>	</ABBREV>	Abbreviations in text
<ACRONYM>	</ACRONYM>	Acronyms in text
<ARG>	</ARG>	Command argument
<CMD>	</CMD>	Command name
<DFN>	</DFN>	Defines a specified term
<FIG>	</FIG>	Like IMG, but with captions
<FOOTNOTE>	</FOOTNOTE>	Footnotes (pop-up windows)
<LIT>	</LIT>	Literal (preformatted text, but without the <TT> font used)
<MARGIN>	</MARGIN>	Like a footnote
<ONLINE>	</ONLINE>	Text only shown on-line
<PERSON>	</PERSON>	Names of people
<PRINTED>	</PRINTED>	Text only shown in printouts
<Q>	</Q>	Short, in-line quotation
<RENDER>		Specify style mapping
<S>	</S>	Strikethrough text
_		Subscript
[	]	Superscript
<TABLE>	</TABLE>	Specification of a table of data

Some of the HTML+ additions are definitely cool, but many of them seem to be crazy, obfuscating add-ons to HTML. The real proof of the additions will be how many are used when the new HTML+-capable browsers are widely used on the network.

The <TABLE> extension probably is the coolest of all, so it's worth showing how that extension may look when it's fully supported. A document that includes <TABLE> information has its fields denoted by <TH> and <TD> (table header and table data, respectively). A row of information ends with <TR>.

```
<TABLE>
<TH>Month<TH>Sales<TR>
<TD>Jan<TD>503<TR>
<TD>Feb<TD>958<TR>
<TD>Mar<TD>3523<TR>
<TD>Apr<TD>5443<TR>
<TD>May<TD>4938<TR>
<TD>Jun<TD>6421<TR>
<CAPTION>Sales for First Half</CAPTION>
</TABLE>
```

The format of this information looks like the following example:

Month	Sales
Jan	503
Feb	958
Mar	3523
Apr	5443
May	4938
Jun	6421

Sales for First Half

Note that the format for tables that's in the latest release of the Netscape Navigator is slightly different. More powerful, the differing format is also more confusing for HTML authors.

HTML+ also includes support (support that probably should have been present from the beginning) for some additional special characters, shown in Table 12-4.

Table 12-4	Some Symbol Extensions in HTML+
Tag	**Common Meaning**
&cent;	Cent symbol
&copy;	Copyright symbol
&deg;	Degree sign
&iquest;	Inverted (Spanish) question mark
&laquo;	Left angled quotation mark
&micro;	Greek micro character
&middot;	Midline dot, a sort of floating period symbol.
&not;	Negation sign
&para;	Paragraph symbol
&plusmn;	Plus or minus sign
&pound;	British pound symbol
&raquo;	Right angled quotation mark
&reg;	Registered-trademark symbol
&sect;	Section sign
&yen;	Yen symbol

The extensions and additions scheduled for HTML 3 are a little harder to identify, because the specification was still being finalized when this book was written. Many of the changes are continued refinements to the HTML+ specifications, including the `<TABLE>` and `<FIG>` tags. The complexity level increases dramatically with style sheets and obscure multipart-header information. For example, HTML 3 will support static banners across a set of documents; a `<LINK>` tag for standard button bars and other graphical elements; and a `<NOTE>` tag for cautions, warnings, and other important material.

FOOTNOTE was, obviously, too long: the HTML 3 specification lists FN as offering the same function. Forms are extended to include graphical editor panels (these are called "scribble-on image" in the specification) and file-uploading and audio-input capabilities.

To check on the status of the HTML specifications, visit `http://www.w3.org/hypertext/WWW`.

Happy HTML-ing

That's about it for *Creating Cool Web Pages with HTML*. Having read this far, you are now an official expert on the hypertext markup language. Now all you have to do is go create the coolest new Web pages on the Net.

As you travel the Web and design your own pages, keep in touch; you can always reach me at the e-mail address `taylor@netcom.com` and, of course, you can check out the Creating Cool Web Pages with HTML Web spot at `http://www.mecklerweb.com/~taylor`.

Glossary

To achieve precision in communication, experts and amateurs alike speak in what sounds an awful lot like a secret code. This glossary is a decoder ring of sorts that should help you understand the various mystery words surrounding HTML and the World Wide Web.

anchor

Either a spot in a document that actually links to another place in the document or another document (a hypertext link), or the spot elsewhere in the document that can be quickly reached through a hypertext link.

anonymous FTP

A scheme by which users can retrieve files over the Internet without having an account on the remote system. Usually, the user logs in as *anonymous* and leaves his or her e-mail address as the password.

attribute

An addition to an HTML tag that qualifes or extends the meaning of the tag.

boldface

To set text off with a heavier font; **this text is boldface**.

A

bookmark

A Web URL that's automatically stored by the browser software for easy access later (also see *hotlist*).

browser

Software program such as winWeb, MacWeb, or Netscape that can read and navigate HTML documents. Browsers are the client application that you run on your PC or Mac.

data

The never-ending stream of stuff that appears on the Internet, as differentiated from *information,* which is data that has some meaning or value to the user.

e-mail

Electronic mail — a convenient way to send messages to other users or groups without the hassle of paper or postage stamps.

font

A particular use of a typeface. Bodoni Poster is a typeface, but Bodoni Poster 12-point italic is a font.

FTP (File Transfer Protocol)

The way files are sent and received over the Internet. Typically, a user needs an account on the remote system unless it allows anonymous FTP access (see *anonymous FTP*).

Gopher

A popular information-distribution service based on a hierarchical menu system; often overshadowed by the more sophisticated World Wide Web. The main Gopher site is at the University of Minnesota.

home page

The central or initial document seen by visitors to your Web site. You can have many other Web pages connected to your home page.

hostname

The unique combination of computer and domain name that describes a particular computer on the Internet. For example, `sage.cc.purdue.edu` is a hostname in the Purdue University Computer Center domain. Alternatively, some people believe just the name of the computer itself is its hostname, with all additional information the domain name. That would mean that the same computer would have a hostname of `sage` and a domain name of `cc.purdue.edu`. There's no consensus.

hotlist

A Web URL that is automatically stored by the browser software for easy access later; also known as a collection of *bookmarks*.

HTML (HyperText Markup Language)

The language that is used to define and describe the page layout of documents displayed in a World Wide Web browser. HTML is an application of SGML (Standardized General Markup Language).

HTML tag

A specific formatting instruction within an HTML document. Tags are usually contained within angle brackets, as in `<HTML>`.

HTTP (HyperText Transfer Protocol)

The underlying system whereby Web documents are transferred over the Internet.

hypermedia

Any combination of hypertext and graphics, video, audio, and other media. The World Wide Web is a hypermedia environment because it allows multiple types of media to be used simultaneously in a document.

hypertext

An interconnected web of text information, wherein any given word or phrase may link to another point in the document or to another document.

information

The small subset of data that is actually useful and meaningful to you at the current moment.

inline graphics

Graphics that appear beside the text in a Web page when viewed via a browser (as opposed to graphics that require separate viewer programs).

the Internet

The global network of networks that enable some or all of the following: exchange of e-mail messages, files, Usenet newsgroups, and World Wide Web pages. Also known as the Net.

italics

A typographic convention typically used for emphasis or citations; *this text is italicized.*

link

A word, picture, or other area of a Web page that users can click to move to another spot in the document or to another document.

markup language

A special type of programming language that allows users to describe the desired appearance and structural features of a document.

Mosaic

The original World Wide Web browser program developed at the National Center For Supercomputiong Applications at the University of Illinois. Its release in 1993 sparked the explosive growth of the Web and helped boost interest in the Internet. Many similar software programs to Mosaic — commercial, shareware, and freeware versions for almost any platform — have been developed since Mosaic's release.

the Net

Another term for the *Internet.*

Netscape

A World Wide Web browser developed by Netscape Communications, created by some of the original NCSA Mosaic programmers. Netscape, more formally Netscape Navigator, may be the most popular browser on the Net.

ordered list

A list of items, often numbered, that describe steps in a process (steps 1, 2, 3, and so on).

pointer

A word, picture, or other area that users can click to move to another spot in the document or to another document; same as *link.*

port

A particular "frequency" used to transfer a particular type of information between Internet computers; FTP uses a specific port, whereas HTTP uses another. Somewhat analogous to television channels.

SGML (Standardized General Markup Language)

The markup language that is the parent of HTML. SGML provides a means of defining markup for any number of document types (such as HTML). You don't mark up text in SGML, per se — you mark up text using an application or instance of SGML. HTML is one of those applications.

TCP/IP (Transfer Control Protocol/Internet Protocol)

A system networks use to communicate with each other over the Internet.

telnet

An Internet service that enables users to log on to a remote system and work on it as though they were directly connected to the system on site.

typeface

A particular design of a set of characters and symbols. Times and Courier are common typefaces. A specific size and style of a typeface — Courier 12 point, for example — is known as a *font.*

URL (Uniform Resource Locator)

The standardized way in which any resource is identified within a Web document or to a Web browser. Most URLs consist of the service, host name, and directory path. An example of a URL: `http://www.timeinc.com/time/daily/time/latest.html`.

unordered list

A list of items that have no implied order; commonly, a set of bulleted items.

UNIX

A very powerful operating system that is the object of a lot of criticism and adoration. Probably the most common operating system on the Internet, UNIX has some Internet features built right into it.

World Wide Web

A massive, distributed hypermedia environment that is part of the Internet. Consisting of millions of documents, thousands of sites, and dozens of indexes, the Web is a fluid and often surprising hive of information and activity.

HTML Quick Reference

Once you've learned how to create documents in hypertext markup language, it's inevitable that you'll need to quickly double-check the form of a particular option, the spelling of a tag, or similar. That's why I include this helpful quick reference material.

What's a URL? (Chapter 2)

```
service      ://    hostname (:port)     /      directory (and filename)
```

service can be

http	Hypertext transfer protocol — Web pages
gopher	Gopher server
mailto	E-mail address
telnet	Telnet to a remote system
ftp	FTP file archive
news	Usenet news server

B

Basic HTML (Chapter 3)

`<HTML>`	Begins an HTML-formatted document
`<HEAD>`	Beginning of HTML header info (TITLE, etc.)
`<TITLE>`*text*`</TITLE>`	Specify *text* as the title for this Web page
`</HEAD>`	End of HEAD section
`<BODY>`	Beginning of main HTML text and info
`</BODY>`	End of HTML body
`</HTML>`	Last line of an HTML document

Paragraph Formats (Chapter 3)

`<P>`	Paragraph break
` `	Line break
`<HR>`	Horizontal rule

Character Formatting (Chapter 4)

`<I>`*text*`</I>`	Present *text* in italics
`<B>`*text*`</B>`	Present *text* in bold
`<U>`*text*`</U>`	Present *text* underlined, if supported
`<TT>`*text*`</TT>`	Show *text* in "typewriter" font
`<EM>`*text*`</EM>`	Emphasize *text*, typically italics
`<STRONG>`*text*`</STRONG>`	Show *text* in a strong (typically bold) font

Adding Images (Chapter 8)

```
<IMG
```

`SRC="file or URL"`	Name or URL of the graphics file to include
`ALIGN=alignment`	Aligns subsequent text to TOP, MIDDLE or BOTTOM of image, as specified
`ALT="text"`	Show *text* instead of image for users who cannot display graphics on their screens
`ISMAP`	Mapped image with multiple click spots; must be supported by the server

```
>
```

Hypertext References (Chapter 6)

`<A>`	Anchor, inserts internal (same page) or external (different page or document) hypertext link
`<A HREF="file or URL">`	Hypertext reference
`<A NAME="text tag">`	Anchor within document for jumping to that spot within the Web document
`</A>`	Close tag

Section Headings (Chapter 3)

`<H1>`*text*`</H1>`	Show *text* as a level-one section heading
`<H2>`*text*`</H2>`	Show *text* as a level-two header

HTML supports up to six levels of headings, but in practice anything less than a fourth level section heading is difficult to read...

Lists (Chapter 5)

`<OL>`	Ordered (numbered) list of items
`<LI>`	List item (number if in OL, bullet if in UL)
`</OL>`	End of ordered list
`<UL>`	Unordered (bulleted) list of items
`</UL>`	End of unordered list
`<DL>`	Definition or glossary list
`<DT>`	Definition term
`<DD>`	Definition description
`</DL>`	End of definition or glossary list

Other Cool HTML Tags

`<BLOCKQUOTE>`	Block indented text passage
`</BLOCKQUOTE>`	End of BLOCKQUOTE passage
`<PRE>`	Preformatted text passage; not filled or altered
`<PRE WIDTH=x>`	Default line width of preformatted text where 'x' specifies the max number of characters to display on each line (ignored by most browsers)
`</PRE>`	End of preformatted text block
`<ADDRESS>`	Signature block at end of HTML page containing contact info for the person who created or maintains the page
`</ADDRESS>`	end of ADDRESS listing

`<DIR>`	Directory listing, a short form of a list (rarely supported)
`</DIR>`	End of DIR listing
`<MENU>`	A list of small items; may be formatted multi-column by the browser software (rarely supported)
`</MENU>`	End of MENU listing
`<!-text ->`	*text* is a comment; not displayed

Building Forms (Chapter 12)

`<FORM>`	HTML form specification header
`<FORM ACTION="file or URL">`	What will process the results
`<FORM METHOD="method">`	How form info is sent - POST is as data, GET is attached to URL
`<INPUT TYPE=TEXT>`	Text input box
`<INPUT TYPE=RADIO>`	One of a group of on-off buttons
`<INPUT TYPE=SUBMIT>`	The actual 'submit form' button
`<INPUT TYPE=RESET>`	Another button for clearing all values entered
`<INPUT TYPE=PASSWORD>`	A text input box that doesn't echo what's typed
`<INPUT TYPE=CHECKBOX>`	An on-off option field

Within an INPUT specification, the following options have value, though not all options have meaning with all types of input field.

`NAME=`	symbolic name of field value
`VALUE=`	default value or content of field

CHECKED	button/box checked by default?
SIZE=	number of characters in text field
MAXLENGTH=	max characters accepted (text)
<SELECT	User must choose between a list of select boxes
NAME=	Name of select boxes
SIZE=	How many items to display at once
MULTIPLE=	Okay to select more than one item
>	
<OPTION	an individual check box within SELECT list
SELECTED	make this the default SELECT selection
> *text for selection option*	
</SELECT>	end of SELECT series
<TEXTAREA	multiline text entry field
NAME=	symbolic name of textarea field
ROWS=	number of lines in input space
COLS=	width of input space
> *default text* </TEXTAREA>	
</FORM>	End of HTML form specification
<ISINDEX>	A searchable index — need CGI support on the server

Special Character Codes for HTML Documents (Chapter 5)

Character	HTML Code	Common Meaning
&	&amp;	ampersand
<	&lt;	less than
>	&gt;	greater than
(c)	&copy;	copyright symbol
(r)	&reg;	registered trademark symbol

See Chapter 5 for a more extensive list of special character codes within HTML

Netscape Navigator HTML Extensions (Chapter 9)

<CENTER>	Center a passage of text, graphics or other material in the window
</CENTER>	End of CENTER list
<HR	Horizontal rule
SIZE=	height of the horizontal line, in pixels
WIDTH=	width of the line: pixels or percentage of screen width
ALIGN=	LEFT, CENTER or RIGHT
NOSHADE	Solid rule line, no (default) shading
>	

<OL		Ordered list of items
	TYPE=	A = uppercase alphabetic, a = lowercase alphabetic, I = uppercase Roman numerals, i = lowercase Roman numerals and 1 = digits.
	START=	initial value for the list
>		
<UL		Unordered list
	TYPE=	Type of bullet/mark to use. Possibilities: DISC, CIRCLE, or SQUARE.
>		
<LI		Individual List item
	TYPE=	Bullet type (UL); DISC, CIRCLE or SQUARE
	START=	starting value (OL only)
>		
<BASEFONT		Default font size for text
	SIZE=	Base font size: range 1-7
>		
<FONT		Change font size for subsequent text
	SIZE=	Specify font size: range 1-7
>		
<IMG		Include image or graphic in document

ALIGN=	Lots of additions to alignment options, including some nicknames for the existing alignment options. Total possibilities are: LEFT, RIGHT, TOP, TEXTTOP, MIDDLE, ABSMIDDLE, BASELINE, BOTTOM, ABSBOTTOM. The two important additions: LEFT, RIGHT
WIDTH=	width, in pixels, of image
HEIGHT=	height, in pixels, of image
BORDER=	size of image border, in pixels
VSPACE=	reserved vertical space around graphic, in pixels
HSPACE=	reserved horizontal space around graphic, in pixels

>

<BR   Line break

    CLEAR=   LEFT, RIGHT, ALLbreak wrapped graphic space

>

Index

(continued)

(continued)

MacWeb and winWeb

Your customers, employees, and partners need information — information that helps them make decisions, evaluate problems, and accomplish tasks. The longer it takes them to find the information, the more it costs.

Power and Simplicity

Finding information with EINet client products is as easy as asking for it. And coupled with EINet secure servers, you control the information returned.

With EINet's World-Wide Web (WWW) clients, users don't need to know where information is located.

Users choose what they want to look at. MacWeb and winWeb locate and retrieve it.

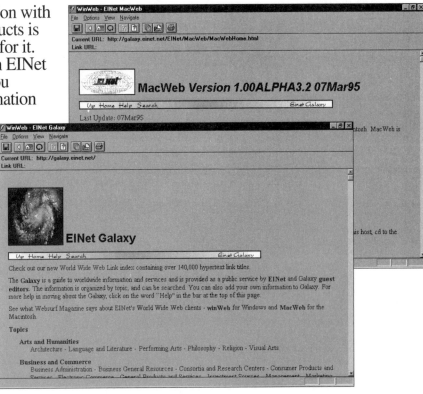

Users don't need to settle for what they can find — instead they can find what they need.

MacWeb and winWeb fully exploit the Web's hypermedia technology while maintaining the look and feel of the operating platform.

EINet Corporation
3500 West Balcones Center Drive
Austin, Texas 78759
Sales and Marketing Department
512-338-3577
512-338-3897 Fax

IDG BOOKS WORLDWIDE
LICENSE AGREEMENT

and your exclusive remedy shall be limited to replacement of the Software, which is returned to IDG with a copy of your receipt. This Limited Warranty is void if failure of the Software has resulted from accident, abuse, or misapplication. Any replacement Software will be warranted for the remainder of the original warranty period or thirty (30) days, whichever is longer.

5. No Other Warranties. To the maximum extent permitted by applicable law, IDG and the author disclaim all other warranties, express or implied, including but not limited to implied warranties of merchantability and fitness for a particular purpose, with respect to the Software, the programs, the source code contained therein and/or the techniques described in this Book. This limited warranty gives you specific legal rights. You may have others which vary from state/jurisdiction to state/jurisdiction.

6. No Liability For Consequential Damages. To the extent permitted by applicable law, in no event shall IDG or the author be liable for any damages whatsoever (including without limitation, damages for loss of business profits, business interruption, loss of business information, or any other pecuniary loss) arising out of the use of or inability to use the Book or the Software, even if IDG has been advised of the possibility of such damages. Because some states/jurisdictions do not allow the exclusion or limitation of liability for consequential or incidental damages, the above limitation may not apply to you.

7. U.S.Government Restricted Rights. Use, duplication, or disclosure of the Software by the U.S. Government is subject to restrictions stated in paragraph (c) (1) (ii) of the Rights in Technical Data and Computer Software clause of DFARS 252.227-7013, and in subparagraphs (a) through (d) of the Commercial Computer — Restricted Rights clause at FAR 52.227-19, and in similar clauses in the NASA FAR supplement, when applicable.

Alternate Disk Format Available. The enclosed disk is in $3^1/_2$" 1.44MB, high-density format. If you have a different-size drive, or a low-density drive, and you cannot arrange to transfer the data to the disk size you need, you can obtain the programs on a low-density, $5^1/_4$" disk by writing to the following address: IDG Books Disk Fulfillment Department, Attn: Creating Cool Web Pages with HTML, IDG Books Worldwide, 7260 Shadeland Station, Indianapolis, IN 46256, or call 800-762-2974. Please specify the size of disk you need, and please allow 3 to 4 weeks for delivery.

EINet License Agreement

winWeb

winWeb is Copyright © 1994 Microelectronics and Computer Technology Corporation (MCC). All Rights Reserved. EINet is a trademark of MCC.

The MCC EINet winWeb Software, both the binary executable and the source code (hereafter, Software), is copyrighted and licensed. MCC provides the Software and licenses its use as set forth herein. The Software is, and at all times shall remain, the property of MCC, and Licensee shall have no right, title or interest therein except as expressly set forth in this agreement. Source code, if made available, will be licensed separately.

MCC grants to Licensee a license to use, copy and distribute the Software for academic, research and personal-use purposes only, without a fee, provided that (i) the above copyright notice and this permission notice appear in all copies of the Software and related documentation, and (ii) the MCC and EINet name may not be used in any advertising or publicity relating to the Software without the specific, prior written permission of MCC, and (iii) that no charge is associated with copies of the Software distributed by Licensee to third parties. Commercial use of this Software is forbidden without the express written permission of MCC and payment of a negotiated license fee.

Licensee may make derivative works. However, if Licensee wishes to distribute any derivative work based on or derived from the Software, then Licensee will (1) notify MCC regarding potential distribution of the derivative work; (2) acquire permission from MCC to distribute the derivative work; and (3) clearly notify users that such a derivative work is a modified version and not the original Software written and distributed by MCC.

Any Licensee wishing to make commercial use of the Software should contact MCC to negotiate an appropriate license for such commercial use. Commercial use includes (1) integration of all or part of the Software into a product for sale or license by or on behalf of Licensee to third parties, or (2) distribution of the Software to third parties that need it to utilize a commercial product sold or licensed by or on behalf of Licensee.

THIS SOFTWARE IS PROVIDED "AS IS" WITHOUT WARRANTY OF ANY KIND, EITHER EXPRESS OR IMPLIED, INCLUDING WITHOUT LIMITATION, THE IMPLIED WARRANTIES OF MERCHANTABILITY OR FITNESS FOR A PARTICULAR PURPOSE. MCC DOES NOT WARRANT THAT THE FUNCTIONS CONTAINED IN

THE SOFTWARE WILL MEET LICENSEE'S REQUIREMENTS OR THAT THE OPERATION OF THE SOFTWARE WILL BE UNINTERRUPTED OR ERROR-FREE. THE ENTIRE RISK AS TO THE QUALITY AND PERFORMANCE OF THE SOFTWARE IS WITH LICENSEE.

IN NO EVENT WILL MCC BE LIABLE TO LICENSEE OR ANY THIRD PARTY FOR ANY DAMAGES, INCLUDING ANY LOST PROFITS, LOST SAVINGS OR OTHER INCIDENTAL, CONSEQUENTIAL OR SPECIAL DAMAGES ARISING OUT OF THE USE OR INABILITY TO USE THE SOFTWARE EVEN IF MCC HAS BEEN ADVISED OF THE POSSIBILITY OF SUCH DAMAGES.

By using or copying the Software, Licensee agrees to abide by the copyright law and all other applicable laws of the U.S. including, but not limited to, export control laws, and the terms of this license. MCC shall have the right to terminate this license immediately by written notice upon Licensee's breach of, or non-compliance with, any of its terms. Licensee may be held legally responsible for any copyright infringement that is caused or encouraged by Licensee's failure to abide by the terms of this license.

Disk Installation Instructions

To install the winWeb browser and accompanying files onto your PC's hard drive, run INSTALL.EXE and follow the instructions.

> Just because you install winWeb on your machine doesn't mean you are "on the Web" or "on the Net." This book does not address issues of signing up with an Internet provider. I assume here that you either already have a SLIP or PPP Internet account and can cruise the World Wide Web or that you merely want to view HTML files on your local machine.

Installing from the disk

1. Insert the disk into your floppy disk drive and double-click on A:/ INSTALL.EXE in File Manager.

   Or select File ⇨ Run in Program Manager, type a:/install.exe in the dialog box, and press Enter.

2. Select the Install Cool Web Pages option in the install program.

3. Select C:/ as the drive you want to install to.

4. Type a new directory name or accept the default C:/COOLWEB.

5. When the install program is finished installing, select Exit installation and click OK.

The install program creates a C:/COOLWEB directory on your hard drive. You should find several .GIF and .HTM files in that directory, along with one .AU file. These files are yours to view, play with, explore, or delete. The .HTM files contain HTML files and can be read with winWeb (which you just installed) or any other browser.

You should also see two subdirectories: C:/COOLWEB/EXAMPLES and C:/ COOLWEB/WINWEB11.

C:/COOLWEB/EXAMPLES contains all the HTML files described in the book. If you see it in the pages of this book, you now have it on your hard drive. These are mostly .HTM (text) files that can be viewed with Notepad and winWeb. Throughout the editing process, these files underwent many changes under tight deadlines. To be sure all the files are error-free, we advise you to obtain and use the latest versions of the files.For updated versions of these files, check out the book's home page at `http://` `www.mecklerweb.com/~taylor/IDG/coolweb.html`.

C:/COOLWEB/WINWEB contains the winWeb program and its associative files. To create an icon for winWeb, arrange File Manager and Program Manager so that you can see the WINWEB.EXE file in File Manager and the program group in which you want winWeb to appear in Program Manager at the same time. Then drag and drop the file WINWEB.EXE from File Manager to the program group in Program Manager and release the mouse button. The icon should appear automatically.

For more information about winWeb, including upgrade information, visit the EINet Web site at `http://www.einet.net`. Also, be sure to read the README.WRL file in the/WINWEB directory.

Note: You will have to place the file VBRUN300.DLL into your Windows/SYSTEM directory and restart Windows (you may already have a copy of this file in there — if so, use the later version and delete the other.)

Also note: winWeb tries to load the EINet home page at `http://www.einet.net/` when you start it up the first time. If you're not connected to your Internet provider at the time, winWeb displays an error message. To change winWeb's home page, select File ⇨ Open and then change to the c:/COOLWEB directory. Double-click on any .HTM file you see. After the file loads, select Options ⇨ Set Home Page..., select Current Page, and then click OK.

IDG BOOKS WORLDWIDE REGISTRATION CARD

RETURN THIS REGISTRATION CARD FOR FREE CATALOG

Title of this book: Creating Cool Web Pages with HTML

My overall rating of this book: ❑ Very good [1] ❑ Good [2] ❑ Satisfactory [3] ❑ Fair [4] ❑ Poor [5]

How I first heard about this book:

❑ Found in bookstore; name: [6]

❑ Advertisement: [8]

❑ Word of mouth; heard about book from friend, co-worker, etc.: [10]

❑ Book review: [7]

❑ Catalog: [9]

❑ Other: [11]

What I liked most about this book:

What I would change, add, delete, etc., in future editions of this book:

Other comments:

Number of computer books I purchase in a year: ❑ 1 [12] ❑ 2-5 [13] ❑ 6-10 [14] ❑ More than 10 [15]

I would characterize my computer skills as: ❑ Beginner [16] ❑ Intermediate [17] ❑ Advanced [18] ❑ Professional [19]

I use ❑ DOS [20] ❑ Windows [21] ❑ OS/2 [22] ❑ Unix [23] ❑ Macintosh [24] ❑ Other: [25]_____
(please specify)

I would be interested in new books on the following subjects:
(please check all that apply, and use the spaces provided to identify specific software)

❑ Word processing: [26]

❑ Data bases: [28]

❑ File Utilities: [30]

❑ Networking: [32]

❑ Other: [34]

❑ Spreadsheets: [27]

❑ Desktop publishing: [29]

❑ Money management: [31]

❑ Programming languages: [33]

I use a PC at (please check all that apply): ❑ home [35] ❑ work [36] ❑ school [37] ❑ other: [38] _____

The disks I prefer to use are ❑ 5.25 [39] ❑ 3.5 [40] ❑ other: [41]_____

I have a CD ROM: ❑ yes [42] ❑ no [43]

I plan to buy or upgrade computer hardware this year: ❑ yes [44] ❑ no [45]

I plan to buy or upgrade computer software this year: ❑ yes [46] ❑ no [47]

Name: _____ Business title: [48] _____ Type of Business: [49] _____

Address (❑ home [50] ❑ work [51]/Company name: _____)

Street/Suite# _____

City [52]/State [53]/Zipcode [54]: _____ Country [55] _____

❑ **I liked this book!** You may quote me by name in future
IDG Books Worldwide promotional materials.

My daytime phone number is _____

IDG BOOKS

THE WORLD OF
COMPUTER
KNOWLEDGE

❑ **YES!**

Please keep me informed about IDG's World of Computer Knowledge.
Send me the latest IDG Books catalog.